TRAINING IN FOOD PROCESSING

TRAINING IN FOOD PROCESSING

Successful approaches

Mike Battcock, Sue Azam-Ali,
Barrie Axtell and Peter Fellows

Practical Action Publishing Ltd
27a Albert Street, Rugby, CV21 2SG, Warwickshire, UK
www.practicalactionpublishing.org

© ITDG Publishing 1998

First published in 1998
Reprinted 2003

ISBN 10: 1 85339 425 4
ISBN 13: 9781853394256
ISBN Library Ebook: 9781780446295
Book DOI: http://dx.doi.org/10.3362/9781780446295

All rights reserved. No part of this publication may be reprinted or reproduced or utilized in any form or by any electronic, mechanical, or other means, now known or hereafter invented, including photocopying and recording, or in any information storage or retrieval system, without the written permission of the publishers.

A catalogue record for this book is available from the British Library.

The authors, contributors and/or editors have asserted their rights under the Copyright Designs and Patents Act 1988 to be identified as authors of their respective contributions.

Since 1974, Practical Action Publishing has published and disseminated books and information in support of international development work throughout the world. Practical Action Publishing is a trading name of Practical Action Publishing Ltd (Company Reg. No. 1159018), the wholly owned publishing company of Practical Action. Practical Action Publishing trades only in support of its parent charity objectives and any profits are covenanted back to Practical Action (Charity Reg. No. 247257, Group VAT Registration No. 880 9924 76).

Typeset by Dorwyn Ltd, Rowlands Castle, Hampshire

Technical Centre for Agricultural and Rural Cooperation (ACP-EU)
The Technical Centre for Agricultural and Rural Cooperation (CTA) was established in 1983 under the Lomé Convention between the ACP (African, Caribbean and Pacific) Group of States and the European Union Member States. Since 2000 it has operated within the framework of the ACP-EC Cotonou Agreement. CTA's tasks are to develop and provide services that improve access to information for agricultural and rural development, and to strengthen the capacity of ACP countries to produce, acquire, exchange and utilise information in this area. CTA's programmes are organised around four principal themes: developing information management and partnership strategies needed for policy formulation and implementation; promoting contact and exchange of experience; providing ACP partners with information on demand; and strengthening their information and communication capacities.

CTA, Postbus 380, 6700 AJ Wageningen, The Netherlands

Contents

THE AUTHORS	vi
PREFACE	vii
1. The importance of food processing training	1
2. Course preparation	8
3. Course implementation	23
4. Monitoring, evaluation and follow-up	46

CASE STUDIES

5. Food processing training in Bangladesh *Shaheda Azami, Sue Azam-Ali and Mike Battcock*	61
6. PRODAR's experience in management training for rural agro-industry – the Central American example *François Boucher and Marvin Blanco*	70
7. Training in food processing – a sustainable approach in India *J.D. John Jayaraj*	75
8. Food processing as a micro-business in Nepal *Sabala Shrestha*	80
9. Training in food processing technologies in Peru *Carmen Rodriguez, Diana Colquichagua, Daniel Rodriguez, Pim Heijster and Walter Rios*	85
10. Fruit processing training in South Africa *Joyene Isaacs, Laetitia Moggee and Phillip C. Fourie*	91
11. Food processing training in Sri Lanka *Vishaka Hidellage*	96
12. Women mean business in Sudan *Abdel Gadir, Sue Azam-Ali and Mike Battcock*	104
13. Food processing training in Uganda *Barrie Axtell, Peter Fellows and Mike Dillon*	111
14. UNIDO training programme for women entrepreneurs in the food processing industry – experiences from Tanzania and Thailand *Gabriele Herrmann and Tezer Ulusay de Groot*	119
BIBLIOGRAPHY	127
INSTITUTIONS THAT SUPPORT SMALL-SCALE FOOD PROCESSING TRAINING	133

The authors

Dr Sue Azam-Ali	Intermediate Technology, The Schumacher Centre for Technology & Development, Bourton Hall, Bourton-on-Dunsmore, Rugby, Warwickshire, CV23 9QZ
Barrie Axtell	Midway Technology Ltd, St Oswald's Barn, Hay on Wye, HR3 5HP, UK
Mike Battcock	Intermediate Technology, The Schumacher Centre for Technology & Development, Bourton Hall, Bourton-on-Dunsmore, Rugby, Warwickshire, CV23 9QZ
Dr Peter Fellows	Midway Technology Ltd, St Oswald's Barn, Hay on Wye, HR3 5HP, UK

The authors acknowledge and would like to thank the following for their important contributions to the case studies:

Marvin Blanco	PRODAR, Sede Central, Apdo. 55-2200, Coranado, Costa Rica
François Boucher	PRODAR, Sede Central, Apdo. 55-2200, Coranado, Costa Rica
Shaheda Azami	Intermediate Technology Bangladesh, GPO Box 3881, Dhaka 1000, Bangladesh
Diana Colquichagua	Intermediate Technology Peru, Casilla Postal 18-0620, Lima 18, Peru
Dr Mike Dillon	Midway Technology Ltd, St Oswald's Barn, Hay on Wye, Herefordshire, HR3 5HP, UK
Phillip C. Fourie	ARC-INFRUITEC, Private Bag X5013, Stellenbosch, Republic of South Africa
Gabriele Herrmann	Odenwaldstr. 4, 61118 Bad Vilbel, Germany
Vishaka Hidellage	Intermediate Technology Sri Lanka, 5 Lionel Edirisinghe Mawatha, Kirulapone, Colombo 5, Sri Lanka
Abdel Gadir Elimam	Intermediate Technology Sudan, PO Box 4172, Khartoum, Sudan
Joyenne Issacs	ARC-INFRUITEC, Private Bag X5013, Stellenbosch, Republic of South Africa
J.D. John Jayaraj	Palmyrah Workers Development Society, Crystal Street, Martandam, 629165, Kanyakumari District, Tamil Nadu, India
Laetitia Moggee	ARC-INFRUITEC, Private Bag X5013, Stellenbosch, Republic of South Africa
Walter Rios	Intermediate Technology Peru, Casilla Postal 18-0620, Lima 18, Peru
Carmen Rodriguez	Intermediate Technology Peru, Casilla Postal 18-0620, Lima 18, Peru
Daniel Rodriguez	Intermediate Technology Peru, Casilla Postal 18-0620, Lima 18, Peru
Sabala Shrestha	Community and Environment Division, Butwal Power Company, Hydro Consult, Pulchowk, PO Box 11728, Nepal
Tezer Ulusay de Groot	United Nations Industrial Development Organization (UNIDO), UN International Centre, A-1400, Vienna, Austria

Preface

Some foods must be processed to make them fit for consumption, to remove toxic compounds and to improve their nutritional value. Other foods are processed in order to extend their shelf-life and to improve food security. Treatments range from relatively simple processes such as rice husking, drying and grinding, to the more complex transformation of oilseeds into margarine and the production of long-life milk.

Processing usually adds value to a foodstuff and is thus a very important means of income generation and employment, particularly in areas where raw materials are readily available. Food processing, therefore, is one of the most important manufacturing sectors in many developing countries.

Characteristics of small-scale food processing

Small-scale food processing responds to local needs and builds on traditional knowledge and skills. It uses local resources and can be owned, managed and maintained locally. By combining well-established principles and appropriate equipment with good standards of quality assurance and hygiene, small enterprises are able to make high-quality, marketable products.

This book is concerned mainly with the provision of training for the small-scale food processing entrepreneur, although some case studies emphasize the importance of processing for home consumption and food security. There are many definitions of micro-, small- and medium-scale enterprises. In this book, the authors have used the following terms:

Microenterprises: employ 1–5 people and have an investment of less than US$500.
Small-scale: employ 5–10 people and have an investment of less than US$5,000.
Medium-scale: employ 10–50 people and have an investment of up to US$50,000.

Each of these scales of production has the following characteristics:

○ easily managed and controlled;
○ uses a high proportion of low-cost, locally available equipment and raw materials;
○ based on and building on indigenous knowledge;
○ dependent on local markets for their products;
○ small capital investment requirements;
○ adaptable to local conditions and changing markets;
○ a small-scale decentralized production which has a smaller negative effect on the environment;
○ generally suitable for women entrepreneurs.

With small firms demonstrating great dynamism and innovation in the industrialized world, increasing interest has been shown in the small-scale sector as a potential motor of economic growth. This is especially true in the context of the stagnation of the large-scale formal sector in much of Africa. Agricultural processing projects conceived in government development plans, or promoted by bilateral aid, have been characterized by a high rate of failure. A substantial proportion of the 'white elephants' in the developing world are officially-sponsored processing plants. A recent UNIDO (United Nations Industrial Development Organization) survey of 204 agri/food plants in the formal sector, in 24 African countries, showed that three-quarters had stopped or were malfunctioning. This may result from poorly designed plants, installed in locations where there is low availability of raw material and/or poor demand for the finished product.

Despite there being numerous opportunities and great potential for small-scale food processors, they have to overcome several disadvantages and constraints. For instance, they have to compete with large businesses, multinational companies and imported food products, all of which have the advantage of economies of scale in their production, and have the financial resources to advertise and diversify their products. This trend is seen increasingly, as trade liberalization policies and deregulation take effect. To compete with these companies, it is essential that small-scale processors produce goods of a consistent quality, with better presentation, if they are to capture markets and survive. To do this, entrepreneurs require access to high-quality training in all aspects of business management and technology development.

Purpose of this book

Skills development in a number of disciplines is an important component of sustainable development of small enterprises. The approaches taken vary according to the individual situation. This book presents a variety of the approaches taken and, more importantly, the lessons learnt in training in small-scale food processing. It is intended that the lessons learnt by these organizations will prove valuable for others who are involved in, or who are embarking on, similar training courses, and allow them to develop successful, sustainable training programmes suitable for their own needs.

The following chapters describe the essential components that need to be addressed to provide successful training programmes. The approach focuses on the trainees as the most important people and the training should be tailored to suit their needs. A number of different types of training are described and supported, where appropriate, by case studies. After examining how adults learn, the book discusses identification of participants' needs and then considers aspects including course length and different learning environments.

1
The importance of food processing training

In development programmes or other forms of assistance, training is a key tool to address the needs of beneficiaries and to achieve the aims and objectives of the programme. Often, but not always, it includes a practical element in addition to theory.

Training is available in any number of disciplines and technical areas, but it is necessary to select the topics that are relevant and of importance to the participants, using a training needs assessment (see Chapter 2). In general there are two broad categories of training: types that are intended to impart specific skills, and types that are intended to raise awareness and encourage group cohesion. Awareness raising is most often used in longer-term development programmes such as improved health, nutrition and food security, whereas skills training can be a component of longer-term programmes or as short, stand-alone courses for entrepreneurs or village groups.

Importance of food processing

The food processing sector is very important for economic development in developing countries. It has become the most important

Small-scale food processing builds on indigenous knowledge and uses locally available materials and equipment (IT/Jean Long)

economic sector in sub-Saharan Africa and is the second most important sector after agriculture in Latin America and South Asia. Small-scale food processing is particularly important for providing sustainable livelihoods for marginalized and vulnerable people in these areas and enables them to increase incomes, employment and food security, as well as improving nutrition and health.

Women play a major role in food processing and marketing (IT/Janet Boston)

Incomes and employment
Food processing provides opportunities for employment and income generation, which is particularly important in many countries because agriculture and the formal sector are unable to absorb growing labour forces. The value added through processing and marketing agricultural products can be much greater than the value of the raw materials themselves. It is estimated that 60 per cent of the labour force of sub-Saharan Africa finds work in small-scale food processing. In Latin America there are at least 5.2 million food processing businesses, employing over 15 million people and, in South Asia, food processing is regarded as the second most important area for employment after agriculture.

Food security
Food processing improves food security by increasing both the availability of, and access to, food throughout the year. The World Bank and the Food and Agriculture Organization (FAO) estimate that around 800 million people still do not have enough to eat on a long-term basis. If those who are not yet free from the fear of hunger are included, this number rises to around 1.2 billion or about one-fifth of the world's population in 1995.

Health and nutrition
The optimum health and nutrition of individuals is dependent upon a regular supply of food and a balanced diet. Food processing can contribute to improved nutrition both directly by making foods more available by preservation, and indirectly through generating income with which to purchase a more varied diet.

However, small-scale food processors face a number of constraints which do not permit them to make the most of the opportunities available. Training is an important means of addressing some of these constraints and can act as a catalyst to both economic development and improved food security and health.

Constraints to small-scale food processing

Skills
Technical skills and knowledge are essential to process foods safely and hygienically, whether they are intended for home consumption or for sale. Additionally if foods are made for sale by small-scale entrepreneurs, a number of additional skills are needed for the successful establishment of food processing businesses. These include technical skills to control processing, quality

Employment prospects can be enhanced by training in food processing (ARC-INFRUITEC)

assurance, business development, marketing, sales and identification of new market opportunities. These management skills are often more important to business success than the skills needed to produce a high quality product.

Access to information

Lack of access to appropriately presented, good quality information is a severe constraint for most small-scale food processors. They are often unaware of technologies that may be appropriate to their needs, even when they are being widely used elsewhere. Other areas of need include:

o information on markets, business management techniques, economic policies, credit arrangements and organizations that provide loans;
o appropriate quality assurance procedures;
o storage techniques; and
o information about equipment, packaging and ingredient suppliers.

Additionally, information about market requirements and product prices, the size of the demand and the quality required are all essential for any entrepreneur. Many small-scale food processors gather information about market demand and prices through word of mouth and informal networks, talking in the market place or tea house. With the rapid changes in scale and sophistication of markets in developing countries, these methods of information gathering and exchange are no longer sufficient and there is a need for training in ways of obtaining information and the provision of information on courses.

Hostile policy environment

The policy environment of many countries in the South is characterized by economic factors such as structural adjustment, export orientation and bias towards large-scale investments. The larger, formal food processing sector may receive government support in the form of subsidies, foreign

Access to information is essential for small businesses. The journal Food Chain *is a useful source of information for food processors (IT/Jean Long)*

exchange allowances, price stabilization, guarantees and access to specialist advice. In contrast, the small-scale informal sector has no political influence, despite its combined voting power, and is therefore subject to the vagaries of national and international economic climates. Training programmes can be used to raise awareness about some of these issues and formulate approaches to address them.

Credit

Access to credit by processors is pivotal in ensuring the success of many small businesses. However, many processors experience difficulties with securing credit and it is one of the most commonly cited constraints. The majority of processors, and in particular women, face problems when seeking credit because of government policies, lack of information, lack of collateral and prejudices against them. These combine to ensure that gaining access to credit is, for some, an insurmountable hurdle. Training programmes can be used to advise entrepreneurs and can assist with the development of a business plan which will facilitate access to credit. Equipped with new skills, entrepreneurs are viewed by the lending agency as more credit worthy and may be heard more sympathetically about arranging a loan or credit.

The role of training

The constraints faced by small-scale processors are therefore many and varied. Well-planned, appropriate training can help to address many of them. Some small-scale processors already have the basic skills to carry out their business, but training can greatly assist them to make high-quality, marketable products. The need for training depends on the type of business, the existing skill level and knowledge of the entrepreneur and staff. The following are examples of commonly expressed training needs:

- specific food technologies;
- use of machinery and plant maintenance;
- local manufacture of equipment;
- hygiene;
- quality assurance;
- new product development;
- packaging and labelling;
- marketing and advertising;
- business management;
- financial management;
- food legislation; and
- safety.

The new food processor has many skills to learn, including packaging and marketing, in order to compete with the established businesses (IT/Mike Battcock)

Training may be used to address one of these specific topics or it may be a complete package, designed to improve the food processing business. Examples of each are included in the case studies.

How adults learn

An understanding of how adults learn will help with the design and implementation of individual training courses. Naturally, the content and the style of teaching on courses differs according to the specific objectives and the type of participants. The scope of this book does not allow for a comprehensive review of the theory of learning, but texts are described in the Bibliography for readers wishing to pursue this topic further.

Before describing how adults learn, a brief insight into why adults want to learn is useful. The motivation behind most adults attending a training course is that they hope to better themselves, either through self-development or through a promotion in their work. The majority of adults will be at training courses because they have chosen to be there. Most courses will (and should) charge a fee which increases the value of the training and encourages commitment to learn. The issue of charging for training is covered in more detail in Chapter 2.

Trainers should ensure that they meet the needs of their students and design courses which are appropriate to their individual situations. For many adult trainees, this is a major investment in time and money, which should be taken seriously by the trainer. The basis of learning in adults is not too different from that in children – strong motivation combined with plenty of activity. However, the trainer will have to make allowances for the inevitable changes which occur as a result of ageing. Ageing affects intellectual and manual performance which in turn can affect both the ability and the pace at which a person learns. As age increases, memory decreases, but this varies greatly between individuals. As a consequence, adults seem to learn best when they do not have to rely on memory, but learn through activity at their own pace, with material that seems relevant to their daily lives and their own experiences.

If the way adults are taught is geared to their own particular needs and interests, they can learn as efficiently as young people. The different ways of learning can be divided into three categories:

○ by activity;
○ by using relevant and realistic material;
○ by using experience.

Learning by activity

Adults learn best by 'doing' rather than by watching or listening. Therefore, it is imperative that training courses contain plenty of hands-on activities. Obviously, there are some elements of training which are inappropriate for practical activity, and in these instances methods should be sought to transfer the information in the most appropriate way. Games can be used (see later section on realistic and relevant material) to transfer this type of theoretical information.

Because short-term memory is weaker in older people, the trainer should cut down on

The trainer needs to introduce new ideas gradually, monitor and change the pace of the course to suit the trainees and allow plenty of time for new ideas, concepts and methods to be assimilated. It is pointless for the trainer to load the trainees with too many facts at once as they will not be registered. Time should be allocated for the trainees to share their experiences as this is a valuable way to learn from others and to boost their confidence. The trainer has to remember to stand back and allow others to speak and share their experiences. The trainer should act as a facilitator for constructive discussion and sharing of ideas, while at the same time ensuring that the key learning points of the session/day are received.

Adults may recall their (often negative) experiences of learning at school where they were lectured at by their teachers with no opportunity for discussion or interaction. The trainer has to overcome these psychological barriers and encourage the trainees to talk and share their ideas.

Written instructions for a certain methodology can be given to literate students for them to work through at their own pace. Obviously, this approach does not work for illiterate trainees. The trainer needs to take great care over the style of writing the instructions. They should be written in a series of numbered steps and in the active rather than the passive tense.

Most courses, like this one run by IT Sudan, involve a large proportion of practical work (IT/Mohammed Majzoub)

the amount of memorizing which has to be achieved. Trainees should be allowed to work at their own individual pace. The trainer should not encourage competition between participants as the pace of learning varies greatly between individuals. This is more likely to dishearten the slower participants and to lower their levels of confidence. For slower learners, taking the plunge to enrol on a training course may be daunting. They may fear that they will be treated like children or made to look foolish in front of their colleagues. The trainer must not, therefore, introduce activities which force the trainees to feel uncomfortable. Adults should measure their progress against their own previous performance rather than comparing it with a rival.

Learning by using relevant and realistic material

Adults find difficulty with what is called 'translation processes'. That is, they find it difficult to transfer what they learn through reading and writing into practical 'hands-on' activity. The best way to learn a manual task is to start by practising it. Reading, writing and watching demonstrations have been shown to delay the learning process as they may introduce confusion.

When a method such as role play is used to illustrate a point, it should be as realistic as possible (even to the point of using real money for exercises involving cash) or adults will view them as childish and a waste of time.

Learning by using experiences
Older people have a wealth of experience which can have both beneficial and negative effects on the learning process. On the negative side, inappropriate methods may have to be un-learnt according to the new training schedule. It is difficult to forget old habits which have been acquired over a life-time. On the positive side, the wealth of experiences (both good and bad) can be used to put new information into context.

Giving back the results
Finding out straight away whether an answer is correct is one of the most important features of learning. People will improve their learning more quickly if they know the results of their attempts and where to make improvements. As a consequence, trainers need to develop effective and speedy means of evaluating trainees' work and feeding back the results to them.

Reinforcement
Frequent practice is necessary to reinforce what has been learnt. Constant reference should be made by the trainer to facts or skills which have already been learnt. The best way to do this is to break up the information into small, easy-to-digest pieces of information.

The attention span of adults is generally quite short. Learning is accomplished more easily by taking frequent breaks or changes in activity. Ideally, the pattern would be from 20 to 40 minutes of learning interspersed by breaks of between five and ten minutes. However, in reality it is difficult to follow this pattern and breaks should be taken where appropriate. When planning sessions the trainer should keep this in mind and not overload the students with too much information.

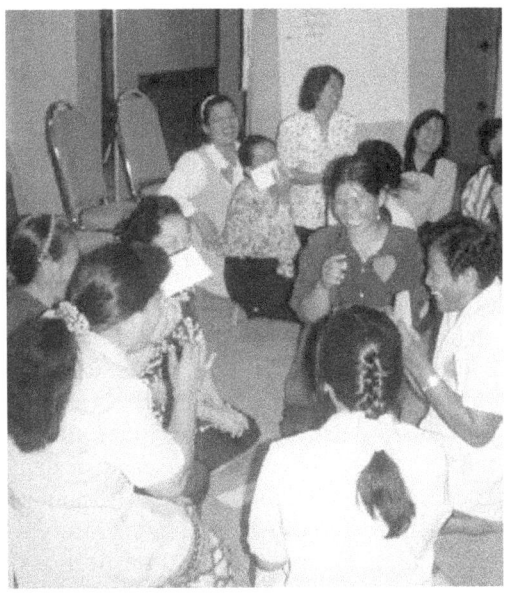
Women in Thailand enjoying a role-play exercise on the training course (G. Herrmann)

2
Course preparation

Training needs identification

In formal education, a course is designed, a syllabus is prepared and students are found to fill the places. In contrast, the starting point when designing a training programme is to clearly identify the specific training needs of the likely participants and design the course to meet those needs. Although trainers have their own individual preferences and areas of skill, and institutions have their own objectives, these should be subsidiary to the needs of participants. Every effort should be made to tailor each course to meet participants' needs rather than those of the training organization.

There are several methods of determining training needs. At the basic level, a sector survey can be carried out to gain a full understanding of the particular sector, to identify constraints and to determine whether training, in one or more disciplines, could solve any of the problems. This approach was adopted by Intermediate Technology in Bangladesh where a survey of the agro-processing sector revealed that there was a serious lack of training in the informal sector for small-scale food processors. Universities offered courses in food science, but these were irrelevant and inappropriate for the small-scale processor. With a knowledge of where the gaps are, it is possible to establish a training course to meet the specific needs.

A second approach to determining training needs is to canvass the ideas of prospective participants. A reputable centre or organization offering training may be approached by prospective trainees with requests for training in their particular areas. The organization can then design a suitable training course to fulfil those needs.

Before planning and designing a training programme, it is necessary to identify the training needs of prospective participants as precisely as possible. When designing a training course, the implementing organization must address the following three questions:

○ What is the purpose of the training?
○ What do likely participants need to learn?
○ How much time and money is available?

To answer these questions it is necessary to have a clear picture of who the participants are likely to be and to ask them what it is they want to learn. They may be extension workers, entrepreneurs, company employees, trainers, members of farmers' co-operatives or women's groups. Each of these types of participant are described in the case studies. For example the case study from Sudan focuses on women's groups who wish to preserve foods for improved food security (see Chapter 12), whereas in Uganda the focus is on small- and medium-scale entrepreneurs who wish to expand their enterprises (see Chapter 13). Institutions and companies that send participants for training are also likely to have clear expectations of the benefits they require, which may differ from those of the participants. These requirements or differences should be taken into account when designing a course.

Training needs assessment

The information required to design an appropriate course (training needs and most suitable course length and venue) is gained by conducting a training needs assessment. Ideally, this should be done before every training programme and the assessment should be carried out by the trainer who will teach the participants, rather than other staff in an organization or institution.

What type of information is required?
The identification of subject areas for training is the first step. Examples of people's perceived training needs could include the following:

o learn how to make specific foods/learn a new processing technology;
o learn how to operate a business making a known range of foods;
o learn how to teach other people to make high-quality foods; and
o learn how to store foods safely.

This is then followed by the collection of other information that is needed to plan a training programme. Examples include:

o the time that participants have available for training;
o the best location for training;
o the levels of literacy and numeracy or educational qualifications; and
o the funds that are available.

Some participants, such as farmers or those already in business, may prefer to have training organized in half-day sessions or one day per week, to enable them to continue their work without being away for long periods. People who have to travel away from home for training may prefer to have longer courses in blocks of one or two weeks, to reduce travelling time and cost. Yet others may not be available at certain times of the year because of other commitments, such as at sowing time, harvest time and religious festivals.

How to assess training needs
The approach to assessment of training needs will differ depending on who is to be trained. If the prospective participants have themselves decided that they need training, they are already motivated and willing to tell the trainer of their needs. Under these circumstances, informal discussions can be conducted within an hour or two with a group of intended participants, such as entrepreneurs, farmers or members of a co-operative or women's group, covering the problems that they are facing, the types of information that they believe will assist them to solve their problems, and their availability for training. The discussions will

Community discussions to determine training needs (IT/Keith Machell)

result in more focused and detailed information than can be obtained by written questionnaires. This approach is described in case studies from Sri Lanka (Chapter 11), Nepal (Chapter 8), Sudan (Chapter 12) and Peru (Chapter 9).

If the target participants are widely scattered in rural areas or live a considerable distance from the trainer, the assessment can be done more cheaply by preparing a questionnaire and sending it to participants for them to fill in and return. However, this method has a number of problems:

o it is of no use if potential participants are not literate;
o it is likely to result in a low return rate;
o unless the questions are carefully designed to be easily understood, there are likely to be some incorrectly answered questions and a need for subsequent clarification; and
o the trainer does not have a clear picture of the potential participants, their work context or the facilities available to them.

A sample questionnaire for a postal needs assessment is shown in Figure 2.1.

Another method of conducting a training needs assessment is to visit likely participants, to see the work that they are doing and their working environment. On such visits, the required information can be gained by discussions and observations with prospective trainees. Although often more expensive, this enables the trainer to adapt materials to suit the participants' particular circumstances and thus make the training more appropriate to their needs. In some instances, it may be more appropriate to design more than one training course in order to meet the needs of all potential students.

A further way in which training needs can be assessed is to form networks of organizations having similar development objectives. In this way an organization that employs field workers or one that is based in a rural area and fully understands the needs of its beneficiaries, can be asked to conduct an assessment on behalf of the training institution. This approach has been successfully used in the case studies from Peru, Sri Lanka and Nepal. In the case study from Uganda (Chapter 13), a similar approach was used in which a manufacturers' association helped to identify the training needs of food processing companies.

It is not necessary to have a formal questionnaire to conduct a training needs assessment, although a checklist of questions can be helpful when interviewing to ensure that all relevant information is collected and nothing is forgotten.

Training audits

In other instances, a small- or medium-scale entrepreneur may have identified problems in the business or wish to introduce a new production technology. There is then a need to improve staff skills or knowledge and provide company-specific training for these staff by a consultant trainer. Here the trainer should adopt an audit approach and watch the staff at work to analyse their skills or shortcomings to decide the training needs. This type of training audit is more time consuming and expensive than the previous methods. The first stage of an audit is to decide the key activities and essential knowledge workers require to carry out their jobs. These can then be summarized as a table (e.g. Figure 2.2) which shows at a glance where training is most needed.

This type of rating can be used to determine each individual's capabilities in the key activities required in their job, the knowledge and skills that are needed and the attitude of each person to their job. Particular indications of lack of ability or poor attitude can be underlined for later inclusion in training needs.

A secondary, but important question concerns any changes that are likely to occur in their work. The above approach takes a 'snapshot' of the current situation regarding training needs, but it also looks ahead to see if any changes in systems, procedures or technologies are likely and decides what training is needed to accommodate these changes. It is possible to orient the training

Please answer the questions below and return the form to the address overleaf:

Name .... Organization ....
Address ....
....
Position .... Tel. ....

1. What types of training are you interested in having? (please tick)
    learning how to store foods safely ☐
    learning how to have better nutrition ☐
    learning how to make a specific processed food ☐
        Which foods are you interested in?
        ....
        ....
        ....

    learning a new processing technology ☐
        Which processes are you interested in?
        ....
        ....
        ....

    learning how to operate a food processing business ☐
    learning how to teach other people to process or store foods ☐
2. How many people would like to receive training? ....
3. What work do they do at present? ....
   ....
4. Where should the training take place? ....
5. When would be a good time for the training? (please circle the months that would be good)
    Jan Feb Mar Apr May June July Aug Sept Oct Nov Dec
6. How long can most people attend a training course?
    Half a day ☐
    Full day   ☐
    Full week   ☐
7. What is the maximum that most people can pay for each day's training?
   ....

Figure 2.1 *A sample postal questionnaire for assessing training needs*

Key tasks	Name 1	Name 2	Name 3	Name 4
1. Know raw material quality standards	*	*	**	*
2. Safe use of slicer	##*	N/A	N/A	##*
3. Knowledge of hygiene	**	**	**	***
4. Record keeping skills	#	#	#	**
5. Control of petty cash	**	***	*	**

Key: * = not up to standard but important in the future   ** = good but could improve   *** = excellent performance   # = not done now   ## = tasks that are critical to the job

Figure 2.2 *Example of a training assessment record sheet*

Name	What (skill/ knowledge required)?	How (training method to be used)?	Where (on/off job, venue)?	When (date and duration of training)?	Why (what are expected benefits of training)?

Figure 2.3 *Summary plan for training*

so that it enables people to cope with future changes in their work. It is then possible to work with each individual in turn, using the assessment, to identify their specific training needs and then draw up a plan of training that covers all identified needs (Figure 2.3).

Once agreed, this can then be used to plan and cost the training programme, optimizing the trainer's time by grouping participants together for sessions that meet specific needs. Participants' time can also be optimized by spreading training sessions using a length and frequency of training that, within limits, best suits them. It may be possible that participants from several organizations can be brought together on specific sessions to make the training more cost-effective.

Selection of participants

The participants are the most important attributes of a training course. Without their involvement, the course cannot take place. The success or failure of the training depends, to a large extent, on selection of the most appropriate participants. Because all training courses are different and the participants potentially have very different needs, they should be carefully selected to ensure they get the most out of the training. Although there are no hard and fast rules about the qualities of a suitable participant, a few general guidelines can be followed:

○ All participants should be of a similar academic level. It is inappropriate to mix people of different levels of literacy and numeracy.

○ Separate courses should be planned for trainers, potential small-scale processors and existing entrepreneurs as their needs and expectations will be very different. As a general rule it is not advisable to mix entrepreneurs and process workers

Colourful posters can be used to attract participants (IT Sri Lanka)

on the same course as extension officers and trainers, because their requirements and expectations from the course are likely to be different. It is interesting to note that in all of the case studies described in this book, training of entrepreneurs and extension workers or trainers, is conducted separately.

o Intended participants should show a commitment to put their learning into practice after completion of the course.
o Where individuals are sent by their employer or development organization, the sending organization must demonstrate that it has the capacity to support the trainees, both technically and financially,

after completion of the course. In some cases, such as the training of trainers programme in Sri Lanka, selection criteria include the capability of the sending institution to support the participant after training.

The importance of ensuring that the course meets the needs of the participants has been stressed, but it is equally important that the participants meet the needs, as specified by minimum entry requirements or other criteria, of the course. If the course objectives are clearly defined, it is a simple step to define the types of participants that would be suitable and the qualifications and experience that are required for participants to benefit most from the training. For example, if the course is intended to develop processing skills, participants should be familiar with the process in question, as a minimum requirement. If the course is intended to make food processing extension officers more effective in their work, the participants should have a minimum number of years' experience of working in this capacity. With most types of training, it is necessary to apply some form of entry requirement and the course organizers need to exercise rigorous selection criteria and choose the best applicants for the places available.

It is important that trainers are involved in the selection of participants that are recommended by other organizations, to avoid risks of preferential treatments and nepotism. Ideally, prospective participants should be interviewed to better understand their backgrounds, and on some courses this is an opportunity to ask participants to bring samples of their products, or information about their businesses, to the course.

Charging for training

It is pertinent to discuss the issue of course fees here. Although many organizations may wish to offer training at a reduced cost or free of charge, it is not advisable to do so. The reasons for this are as follows:

○ If there is a fee for the training, only those who are seriously committed will attend (unless money is not a problem and in this instance the course organizers need to filter out those who are not serious).
○ Training that is offered free of charge reduces the value of the training and may attract individuals who are mainly concerned with collecting certificates. Where funds permit, it may be possible to reimburse participants for expenses.
○ On no account should participants be paid to attend the course as this will attract people for the wrong reasons.
○ As a minimum, courses should aim to cover their costs. Obviously this will be impossible to achieve if the participants are paid to attend.

Costs of training

All training programmes, whether conducted as subsidized activities of an institution or held as a self-financing activity, should be monitored and controlled financially. In the case of institutions that have a budget for training, proper monitoring and control of costs can help to increase the range and quality of courses that are offered. When training is conducted as part of a larger development programme, the control of costs is essential both to setting appropriate course fees and to remaining within overall budgets.

Identifying costs

There are different ways in which the costs of a training programme can be accounted for. A common approach is to use cost centres such as:

○ trainer's fees;
○ course materials (including foods for practical work, purchase of books and photocopying);
○ venue hire;
○ equipment hire or purchase;
○ participants' meals and accommodation;
○ telephone, fax and postage;

Equipment hire or purchase is only one of many costs of running a food processing training course (IT)

- contribution to administrative costs and overheads;
- course promotion;
- travel;
- evaluator's costs; and
- closing ceremony and certificates.

In this method a budget can be set for each cost centre and all expenditure is allocated to one of the centres. If the costs under any budget heading are likely to over-run, the trainer or management team then take decisions on whether to increase the overall budget, cancel further activity under that budget or transfer money between headings. The aim is to ensure that all costs are monitored and controlled and that the total amount spent does not exceed the training budget. At the end of the training, each cost centre can be examined to find where potential savings can be made on subsequent courses.

In a second system, the different aspects of providing training are separately identified and an overall budget for each activity is allocated. For example the following activities could be included:

- course development costs;
- promotion costs;
- participant recruitment costs;
- course implementation costs; and
- monitoring and evaluation costs.

Course development costs include fees for the course manager or consultants to conduct a training needs assessment, design the course structure and content, travel to visit potential participants, briefing resource persons and other trainers, preparation of course materials (including typist's time and photocopying) and visiting suppliers of equipment and materials.

Promotion costs include designer's time and printing costs for a course brochure that can be distributed to sending organizations, postage costs, newspaper, radio or other advertising costs.

Participant recruitment costs may include travel costs if asked to attend an interview, fees for trainers involved with participant selection and administrator's time for correspondence with applicants, registration procedures, etc. These costs are more likely to be incurred on longer courses or international courses where administration is more complex and time consuming.

Course implementation costs include fees for trainers and resource persons, all course materials, venue hire, equipment hire or purchase (note that the cost of equipment would normally be spread over several courses), travel to visit factories, farms, etc., participants' food and accommodation, certificates and refreshments for the closing ceremony.

Monitoring and evaluation costs can be separated into routine course monitoring, which may be included as an implementation cost, and evaluation costs, where a separate follow-up exercise is held to assess the impact of the training.

Administration of income and expenditure
One person should be given responsibility for setting up administrative systems to record all income and expenditure on a training programme. The systems should be transparent, easily understood by everyone who is involved and readily available for inspection. Authorization for all expenditure should be clearly defined from the outset and should ideally rest with the course organizer.

The administrative procedures that are normally required include:

- opening a bank account or a subsidiary ledger or account to deal with all income and expenditure;
- recording all expenditure headings in a ledger and maintaining the ledger on a daily basis;
- checking expenditure against budget headings weekly and producing weekly or monthly summaries, depending on the complexity and duration of the courses; and
- introducing a system of authorization for use of petty cash to buy incidental items during a course.

Setting course fees
If a course is intended to be self-financing, the total estimated costs above are divided by the target number of participants to obtain the cost per participant (i.e. the maximum course fee). Alternatively, if a fixed sum is available to fund each participant, perhaps through a training grant, the total cost of the course is divided by the funds available to give the number of participants required for the course to break even.

These crude calculations do not take any account of the more complex situations that are faced by most trainers, including the provision of financial support by other organizations to train their own staff, manufacturers who may supply materials free of charge, or the use of variable fee rates that depend in part on the ability of participants to pay the full amount. Some funders have a maximum grant per participant whereas others have a target number of people to assist with training each year. In the last case, the costs of a training course may be compared by funders to other courses and decisions made on the basis of cost rather than the benefits of the different training opportunities.

Participants' ability to pay
The costs involved in training are related to a large extent to the funding arrangements for the training programme and any subsidy that is available. In general, for training programmes to be sustainable, it is highly preferable for participants to contribute part of the cost of training and in some programmes (e.g. Uganda case study, Chapter 13), the aim is to achieve full cost recovery from participants' fees. Under no circumstances should participants be paid to attend training programmes. In most societies people attach more value to something that they have to pay for. Therefore, paying participants to attend a course devalues the training. Additionally, paying participants distorts both the reasons why some people attend and the group dynamics, leaving the potential of other participants adversely affected. These attitudes interfere with the successful provision of training and develop a focus on the financial gains that can be made.

It is recognized that, when training poor people, there is often insufficient income available in families to cover the costs of a professionally run training programme. In addition, the opportunity cost of losing income from work while attending a course may deter some participants. In these circumstances, provided participants see the benefits of training as being greater than the costs involved to them (not only direct costs and opportunity costs but also making arrangements for child care and travelling costs), they will attend. Fees should be set at a rate that is affordable (for example, the equivalent of one day's income for a week-long course) and the balance subsidized by the funders.

There is a broad distinction operating in many countries between training for social and health improvement and training for

Participation will only be possible for some trainees if the course is held locally rather than in an urban centre (IT/Mohammed Majzoub)

enterprise development. In the first category, improved food security and nutrition, better hygiene in food preparation and encouragement of the formation of producer groups among poor people, has often been funded by government and non-government programmes as a component of community or integrated rural development programmes. Here the objectives of training are seen as long-term social and welfare improvement. In contrast, such agencies and institutions have often not supported training for commercial food enterprise development, as it is seen as non-egalitarian and likely to further increase divisions between the poor and wealthy.

The view for many years has been that enterprises should be able to pay for staff training from their profits. This view is changing among some funders who realize that small enterprises create employment, which in turn has a significant role in reducing poverty and ill health. Micro- and small-enterprise development programmes now operate in many developing countries, and training for owners, managers and staff is seen as an important means of encouraging long-term sustainable development.

These programmes are, therefore, important sources of subsidy for training in food processing. Other forms of subsidy for training are also being investigated by some organizations, including donations, in kind or paid advertisements on training materials from larger manufacturers as part of marketing strategy, and the sale of goods and services by the training organization to provide income for training subsidies.

Course design

The objectives of a training course and the needs of participants will determine the design and course content. It is unlikely that two courses with the same overall objectives will ever be identical because the needs of the participants will strongly influence the direction and pace of delivery of a course. When designing a training course, the trainer must build in a degree of flexibility to allow for different speeds in learning and for repetition of exercises and concepts which are difficult to grasp. When designing the individual course components and timing of the sessions, the trainer must take into account the learning capabilities of the group. Ideally, training courses should contain a balance of theory and practice, with a higher percentage of practice, since adults learn better by doing than by listening or watching. The trainer should also take care not to be over-ambitious with respect to the amount of material and number of facts which can be learnt at one time. It is a common fault for trainers to attempt to cover too much in one session. Sufficient time should be allowed for students to repeat the methods they have learnt and for breaks between sessions to allow the information to sink in. Time should also be allocated for discussion and problem sharing.

It is possible to identify four general types of course that are based on the different backgrounds and different requirements and expectations of participants. These are summarized in Table 2.1, together with the specific advantages and limitations of each type.

Type of course	Type(s) of participants	Specific advantages	Specific limitations
International (participants from all over the world)	Trainers or extension workers	Exchange of ideas and experiences by qualified technical people. Focus on training methodologies and 'new' technical ideas.	Detailed economic and legislative environments or problems facing food processing sector are difficult to discuss because of variations between countries. Little detailed practical information can be used to assist practitioners.
Regional (participants from neighbouring countries)	Extension workers, trainers, experienced entrepreneurs	Focus on regional issues, regional foods and economic environments.	Limited exchange of new ideas and experience from outside the region in question. Lack of detailed information, although less so than for international courses.
National (participants from one country)	Extension workers, trainers, new or existing entrepreneurs	Detailed information can be provided on sources of equipment, materials, sources of funding, government assistance to small enterprises, public health legislation, export credits. Course highly focused and relevant.	Little exchange of new ideas from outside the country.
District (participants from neighbouring areas within a country)	New or experienced entrepreneurs or household-level processors.	Fewer problems of travelling away from home or work. Very detailed practical information can be given that is specific to a few product groups or a local area.	Difficulty in selecting training methods for more advanced concepts that may be important but are not seen by participants as being directly relevant (e.g. bookkeeping, marketing, microbial spoilage). Very little exchange of new ideas from outside the area.

Table 2.1 *Some advantages and limitations of different types of course*

International courses offer good opportunities for exchange of ideas and experiences and they enable participants to get a different perspective on their own work, away from the pressures of their job and their normal working environment. However, because of the widely differing circumstances in different countries, it is not usually possible to go into detail about specific aspects such as legislation, economic factors or social conditions and as a result there is a danger of this type of training becoming a 'talking shop' with little practical assistance being made available. Trainers on this type of programme should make every effort to ensure that detailed, practical information is made available as either handouts, publications or contact lists for participants to follow up after the training.

Similar problems apply on *regional* training courses, although they are fewer because of the geographical proximity and in most cases, cultural and economic similarities. In some areas, including South-east Asia, Central America and East Africa, where concerted political and economic efforts are being made to integrate countries into regional groupings, this type of training can have great benefits. However, it is important for the trainers to ensure that new ideas from outside the region are brought into the course, either through published information

Trainers must ensure that all necessary equipment for the practical sessions is available, well in advance of the course (IT Sri Lanka)

or by using guest trainers or presentations.

National training courses are most useful for practitioners such as field workers or entrepreneurs who can benefit from discussing common problems with similar people from other areas of their country. This type of course is very useful in building networks of people in similar vocations. In the case of entrepreneurs, the distance between participants may often mean that they are not in direct competition for markets and are thus more willing to share experiences and problems. Additionally, because of the more limited geographical spread of participants, they are more likely to face similar problems of equipment and materials supplies, transport or market sizes. They also operate under uniform legislative and economic conditions and it is therefore possible for trainers to provide detailed information on sources of equipment, packaging, food standards and financial aspects, such as interest rates and government incentives. In most countries, this type of training can also be set within a uniform cultural context and thus be highly relevant to participants.

Lastly, *district* training is most suited to participants who are unable or unwilling to travel far from their home or workplace. This type of training has all the benefits of national courses in being highly relevant to participants' needs and applied to their cultural, economic and social contexts, but additionally it is suitable for people who are less confident about being outside their normal social group. The training can be made highly specific to a small geographical area and can focus on detailed local issues that affect participants. The main problem with this type of training when used to train entrepreneurs is the close proximity of both their markets and suppliers and this may result in participants being unwilling to share experiences or information during a course. Additionally, unless the trainer takes specific steps to introduce new ideas using guest speakers or published information, there is a risk that district courses

Activity	Weeks: 1 2 3 4 5 6 7 8 9 10 11 12
1. Training needs assessment	
2. Design of course	
3. Identification/briefing of trainers	
4. Establish course administration	
5. Secure funding	
6. Promotion of course	
7. Prepare course materials	
8. Hire training rooms	
9. Select participants	
10. Hire equipment	
11. Go through practical work with assistants	
12. Prepare equipment and materials	
13. Purchase foods	
14. Course starts	

Figure 2.4 *Sequence of activities from conducting a training needs assessment to holding a course*

become parochial and potential opportunities for collaboration or development of new markets outside of the area are missed.

Sequencing activities after a training needs assessment

A typical timetable for conducting a training needs assessment, designing a course and selecting participants is shown in Figure 2.4, together with the sequence of subsequent activities. There are clearly going to be differences in the length of time between conducting the needs assessment and holding the course, depending on the trainer's familiarity with the participants' backgrounds, other commitments and workload, access to funding and the resources that already exist at the training institution.

As indicated in Figure 2.4, the sequence of activities is normally as follows:

(1) Conduct the training needs assessment and identify the types of participants and the specific training that is required.

(2) Use this information to either design a new course or adapt existing materials to make a suitable programme to meet the identified needs.

(3) Identify who will develop the training materials and conduct the course. If this is not the person who has conducted the training needs assessment, brief the trainer on what is required.

Course participants at the Uganda Manufacturers' Association training centre (Midway Technology)

(4) Set up a register to record participants who have enrolled for the training, fees paid (amount and date), applications for subsidies or grants and biodata of participants. At the same time, if the training requires financial assistance, prepare a funding proposal and make applications to funders.

(5) If training is held several times for similar types of participants, it may be necessary to advertise that the course will take place and request suitably qualified people to apply for registration. This is best done through networks of like-minded organizations or through newspaper or radio advertisements

(6) The designated trainers should then design the detailed training programme, including preparation of trainers' notes, collection of resource materials and background information, testing of equipment and new practical methods with technicians and resource persons. Where necessary, arrangements should be made at this stage to hire any special items of equipment that are required and to secure donations in kind or the loan of equipment and materials from commercial companies or other institutions.

(7) Within a week or two of the start of the course, it is important to review the availability of all materials and equipment and ensure that resource persons (and trainers!) are completely familiar with the content of the sessions, any safety considerations in operating equipment and the location of all materials and other course inputs.

Although the design and preparation described above may appear to be a considerable amount of work, especially for a short course, it has been found in the authors' experience that unless this level of preparation is done, the training will be badly organized and unprofessional and there are likely to be serious problems of satisfaction by participants, particularly if the training involves practical work.

Suitable training environment

It is essential to have a suitable environment for a training course in which participants feel comfortable and relaxed. They will then be more willing to participate and learn. There are often more complaints about unsuitable training environments than about the actual course content.

A training room should be well ventilated, shaded from direct sunlight and quiet. The room should be large enough to accommodate participants working in groups, typically four or five groups of four people. As a minimum, the following facilities are normally required for class work:

○ sufficient tables and chairs;
○ a blackboard or whiteboard;
○ a flipchart, stand and pens;
○ notepads and pens for participants; and
○ a simple first aid kit.

Additional facilities may include an overhead projector, pens and acetates, a video player, a slide projector, blackout facilities and a screen, calculators and access to a photocopier. Facilities for hand washing, toilets and the provision of food and drinks should be close by.

On residential courses, the living accommodation should be clean, secure and sufficiently spacious. It is important, especially on courses for women, that the building is safe and well guarded. In some cases child-care facilities may be required. The food provided on a course does not need to be lavish but should be nutritious and of the type normally eaten by the participants. Poor-quality food is a common area of complaint on training courses. On longer courses, there should be opportunities for leisure activities in the evenings and weekends to help build group cohesion and enthusiasm.

For longer courses, the choice is whether to have a dedicated training centre, as described in the Sri Lankan case study (Chapter 11), or to arrange a training course that can be held at different sites. There are advantages and disadvantages in both approaches: with a dedicated training centre, resources can be spent on permanent facilities, which may include a library, kitchen, accommodation, office and a practical training room. There is no need to ensure new locations are suitable for each new course, nor negotiate and arrange hire charges each time. A permanent training centre also provides a focus and identity to a course.

The disadvantages of a dedicated centre are the capital cost of construction, potentially higher costs for maintenance and repairs, responsibility for security and the need for participants to travel larger distances. Additionally, when training rural people an elaborate facility may make them feel uncomfortable.

With courses that are held in different locations, it is clearly easier to bring the training closer to participants. The local training facility will feel less intimidating than a centre in a distant region. Costs may be lower, but trainers may have additional problems in ensuring that all facilities are appropriate and in place. In rural areas there may also be problems with electricity, drinking water supplies, and adequate accommodation for trainers and participants. The case studies from UNIDO, Sudan and Bangladesh (Chapters 14, 12 and 5 respectively) are examples of training courses that do not use permanent centres but move between different venues. However, in countries that have large differences in ecology and climate, it is important that courses are held in the zone from which participants are drawn and a single centre is not appropriate. Peru is an extreme case, as its climate varies from very cold, high-altitude areas to hot, humid zones in the Amazon basin. For this reason, when Intermediate Technology established projects in Peru, three training centres were established, one in each of the main ecological zones.

The site for the course needs to balance accessibility with sufficient isolation to avoid undue distractions. In Bangladesh, for example, problems have been encountered when people are brought into the capital, Dhaka, due to the distraction of the city and participants leaving the course early to visit relatives or make business contacts.

3
Course implementation

Appropriate training methodologies

As described in Chapter 1, adults learn best *by doing* rather than by listening. It is therefore necessary for trainers to use a range of training techniques that promote active participation, rather than allowing participants to be just passive recipients of information they provide. Trainers should always remember that 'I should be concerned with what participants will learn and not what I will teach'.

The two most important factors in implementing a training programme are first to involve people in active individual or group work and secondly to structure the programme in a way that participants can learn from each other's experience and knowledge – in other words to implement a participative approach to training.

This approach is feared by many trainers either because they are afraid that they may be asked a question to which they do not know the answer (and therefore lose the respect of participants) or because they are not in constant control of the group and cannot predict what will happen during a session. Too frequently a food scientist or technologist is more interested in demonstrating to the trainees how much he or she knows about the subject, rather than listening to what the trainees want to learn. As a result trainees are 'blinded by science' and emerge from the course having learnt little and believing that food processing is a very difficult subject.

The training needs assessment (described in Chapter 2) can be used to guide the trainer in selecting the best course design, content and training methods for the types of participants that are to be trained. However, all participative techniques require trainers to have a level of confidence in their own abilities and a willingness to loosen control of the training session, in order for participants to work in groups and sometimes to 'take the stage' to share experiences and opinions.

Once a trainer has an understanding, from the needs assessment, of the areas to be covered on a course and the depth of knowledge that is required by participants, the next problem is how to implement the training. For trainers to feel confident in using participative training techniques, it is usually necessary for them to undertake a Training of Trainers (TOT) course.

When done properly, this will give trainers a new confidence in their own abilities and encourage them to loosen control of sessions while implementing a well-planned and structured training process. It will also give them a range of new training techniques to add to their armoury which will encourage participation. These outcomes of a TOT course will result in a more relaxed and confident trainer, who is able to guide group discussions, exercises and teamwork that promote better and longer-lasting learning by participants.

A planned and structured use of participative methods will:

○ enable opportunities for participants to think about applying new skills in their work;
○ encourage greater depth of thought;
○ enable participants to have a constructive impact on each other's thinking;
○ provide opportunities for trainers to give individual guidance and support, praise and recognition to participants; and
○ enable participants to feel that they have achieved something themselves.

In this chapter, techniques that are appropriate to participative learning in food processing are described, followed by a brief

Type of activity	Suggested approach
Short, simple activities that require a few minutes	Demonstrate or explain the activity at the start and facilitate/supervise participants until they have completed it
Straightforward activities that take a longer time	Demonstrate or explain the activity in stages, allowing participants to complete each stage before moving to the next
Difficult activities where errors are likely to occur	Explain the activity in stages and allow time for several practice sessions. In each session, carefully review the outcomes to identify and correct errors before repeating the activity until all are confident in reaching the required standard

Table 3.1 *Approaches to three types of activity in a training session*

summary of some potential problems that can arise and their remedies.

Planning a session

When planning a session, it is necessary to focus first on what the participants will be expected to achieve (the objectives of the session) and how well they will be expected to do it (standards to be achieved). Both should be written down clearly. It is then possible to select a sequence of participative techniques that will enable the objectives and standards to be met.

When considering the methods to be used the following general principles are a useful guide:

- Start from what is familiar to participants and move to the unfamiliar.
- Decide what is essential information and what would be 'nice to know'.
- Break the information into easily digestible units.
- Decide the sequence of activities by thinking through likely learning difficulties and the logical sequence of learning.
- Plan the steps needed to achieve a learning objective so that they are not too small (boring and demotivating) and not too large (incomprehensible). If in doubt, plan for larger steps and then break them into smaller steps if participants have difficulty.
- Do not overload participants with information.

Three general methods can be used when planning a sequence of training activities and the suggested approach for each is shown in Table 3.1.

Summary of participative training techniques

Training illiterate people

There are many situations where a demand exists for training in food processing for people who are illiterate. Farmers' groups, street-food vendors, women's groups and many rural people may be unable to participate in 'traditional' training programmes because the techniques used during training place a requirement on them to be able to read and write. Although there have been substantial developments in training illiterate people in agriculture, health, hygiene, family planning and nutrition, there are, to the authors' knowledge, only a few examples of training techniques in food processing that have been specifically developed for illiterate people.

Provided that suitable equipment and facilities exist, practical training in food processing methods poses few problems for

Equipment and materials required
Agar (e.g. malt extract agar)
Petri dishes (or other shallow, covered dishes)
Pressure cooker
Glass bottle, sealed with a wad of cotton wool

Preparation
1. Add 50g agar powder to 1 litre of distilled water in a glass bottle and pressure cook for 15 minutes at 115°C (lower setting or 10lbs per square inch pressure)
2. Allow agar to cool until hot enough to touch
3. Pour into shallow layers (e.g. 0.5cm) in Petri dishes, replace cover and allow to cool to room temperature

Procedures
1. Explain to participants that the agar is food for moulds and other micro-organisms that contaminate foods or cause illness
2. Give a dish to each participant and ask them to touch the agar with their fingers
3. Mark the dishes 'unwashed hands'
4. Ask half the participants to wash their hands in the normal water supply and then touch a second dish of agar
5. Mark the second set of dishes 'water'
6. Ask the other half to scrub their hands using a medicated soap or similar
7. Mark the third set of dishes 'soap'
8. Place all dishes in a warm place (25–30°C) for a day

Results
The 'unwashed' dishes should show profuse microbial growth. 'Water' dishes should be less and 'soap' dishes should have very few spots of growth. Use the results to emphasize the importance of scrubbing hands with soap and clean water before handling foods. The method can be modified to show the effect of using bleach on surfaces or equipment, by wiping them with sterilized damp cotton wool (115°C for 15 mins) and then wiping this over the agar plates.

Figure 3.1 *Method for using microbiological plates to demonstrate good hygiene and sanitation*

The five finger approach has been used in Bangladesh to teach aspects of business management and planning (IT/Alamgeer Haque)

illiterate people: the trainer can demonstrate a process and then supervise participants as they practise the techniques, giving verbal advice and feedback as they work. Similarly, concepts of improved hygiene and sanitation can be demonstrated using microbiological plates (see Figure 3.1), if these facilities exist.

The difficult aspects of training illiterate people arise when considering business subjects, particularly financial management and marketing. At first sight these difficulties appear to be insuperable, but with a little thought and discussion with participants, there are suitable methods that can be used, although the training may take longer than

Flipcharts are used to record and cluster the main ideas generated from a 'hum' group (IT/Ahmed Ali)

with literate participants. For example, it is well known that illiterate food vendors are able to calculate production costs, sales prices, discounts and profitability in their heads as they work. In training courses these skills are developed further by the simple device of using actual money and two trays (one representing cash into the business and one representing payments to suppliers). Similarly when considering markets and market share, a combination of discussions of participants' experience with images drawn on flipcharts to characterize different types of customer can be used to good effect. Images such as pie charts can be used instead of percentages.

Training literate and numerate people
There are other participative techniques that use written materials and are thus suitable only for literate participants. These techniques have specific uses and are used for example to start a session, to change a subject, to deepen participants' understanding, to gain practice and to get their commitment to take action.

Techniques that can be used to start a session or change a subject include:

○ brainstorming;
○ buzz groups;
○ hum groups;
○ question and answer sessions; and
○ tick boxes.

Techniques that are used to deepen participants' understanding include:

○ case studies;
○ exercises;
○ instructional talks;

- instructional visits;
- role play; and
- simulation exercises.

Techniques that are used to gain participants' commitment include:

- action plans; and
- summary techniques.

These methods are used in a sequence throughout each day's training to enable participants to reach the stated objectives in a structured way that builds on existing knowledge and experience. In the following section, each of these methods is summarized and an indication of the likely time required is included (*note*: where 'flipchart' is used, it includes other forms of display, such as blackboards or overhead projectors).

Techniques that can be used to start a session or to change a subject

Brainstorming

This technique is used to introduce or change the subject on a training course, to examine the breadth of a topic or to get a lot of ideas very quickly. It is done in two phases: brainstorming (10 minutes) followed by a link to the next technique. The trainer writes up a subject on the flipchart and asks participants to call out their ideas. For example the trainer could write 'Quality of food' and ask participants what the phrase means to them. All replies should be written up as one- or two-word contributions without questioning or challenging any ideas (for example: 'colour', 'food poisoning', 'value for money'). The aim is to get as much information as possible onto the flipchart within a short time. When all ideas have been exhausted, the trainer can then categorize participants' responses into groups, highlight those that are most important and link the ideas with the topic under discussion. It is a useful technique to focus from the broad areas of a subject down to the specific topic to be discussed next.

Buzz groups

This technique is in two parts: an initial 'buzz' (10 minutes) followed by a discussion (20–30 minutes). The technique involves putting a question on a flipchart and asking participants to work in groups of three or four to produce a written list of points or answers to the question on either a sheet of paper or a flipchart sheet that can be later hung on the wall. Allow them to work together until the 'buzz' stops and then go through the answers that each group has produced, using them to focus a discussion of the topic.

Hum groups

There are three phases in this type of activity: a 'hum' session (5 minutes), a feedback session (5–10 minutes) and a discussion (10–15 minutes). The technique involves putting a question or instruction on a flipchart and asking participants to work in pairs to produce a written list of answers to the question on either a sheet of paper or a flipchart. A typical instruction would be 'Make a list of the three most important features of . . .', or a question may be 'What are the advantages of . . .?' Allow them to work together until the 'hum' stops and then write their answers on a flipchart until everyone has exhausted their lists. The trainer may group the answers in a way that illustrates the next point or topic to be covered, or select the most important points from the flipchart and use them to focus a discussion.

Question and answer sessions

This allows participants to discuss the aspect under consideration in the context of their own experience. It is a useful technique to incorporate into a talk but the expected results of asking the question should be clearly identified beforehand and should link with the next question or the next part of the talk. An initial question should be written into the trainer's notes, such as 'How can this problem be avoided?' After participants have answered, a supplementary question can be asked, such as 'Can anyone see any

	Entrepreneurial characteristics	
☐ 1a. Good entrepreneurs keep lists and write everything down.		☐ 1b. Good entrepreneurs can keep things in their head.
☐ 2a. An effective entrepreneur works longer than the staff.		☐ 2b. Effective entrepreneurs make economies with the effort they expend.
☐ 3a. If something is important it is also urgent.		☐ 3b. Importance and urgency are not the same.
☐ 4a. At the end of the day when there is little time left, it is better to do a small job of low priority.		☐ 4b. It is better to get on with a large important job at the end of a day.
☐ 5a. You cannot be a good entrepreneur unless you have clear objectives.		☐ 5b. Sticking rigidly to objectives does not allow an entrepreneur to react to situations as they arise.

Figure 3.2 *Example of a tick box sheet*

risks in doing that?' or 'What is your experience of doing this, Abdullah?' Additional questions can be asked to ensure that everyone has an opportunity to contribute. The session should then be summarized to bring the main points of the discussion together and link them to the content of the talk or the objective of the session. Normally a question and answer session would last from 5 to 20 minutes.

Tick boxes

Tick boxes allow the trainer to establish participants' knowledge and previous experience and/or to obtain their views on a topic. It consists of handing participants a tick box sheet, explaining what is to be done and asking them to fill in the sheet alone within about five minutes. The trainer then goes through the answers (from 15 to 20 minutes) to obtain participants' experiences of the topic and determine any differences in their views. The trainer should then discuss these differences and draw conclusions to lead into the next part of the session. An example of a tick box sheet is shown in Figure 3.2.

Techniques that are used to deepen participants' understanding

Case studies

Here the trainer prepares a short written description of a set of events to illustrate a series of issues. It can be designed to enable participants to either analyse the causes of a particular problem or to solve a problem (e.g. Figure 3.3). The three parts of using a case study involve participants reading the extract, which should be one to two pages in length (5–10 minutes) followed by an exercise in pairs or groups to discuss the case study in relation to questions posed by the trainer. Finally, there is a discussion of participants' findings by the whole group. Case studies are useful to make an objective examination of a particular issue and to provide opportunities for participants to exchange ideas and information based on their own experiences. They also highlight possible solutions to problems that participants may face in their own work situations.

> *Working in groups of four, identify different types of quality problems that the food producer found and the methods used to overcome the problems.*
>
> **Quality problems**
> Mr Pantos, the manager of RPD Foods received a letter from Premier Sales, one of the main retailers he supplies, saying that there was a noticeable difference in colour between different batches of the pineapple fruit drink he supplied last month. They point out that their customers have enjoyed the product and have expectations that it will be the same for future purchases, but they have been disappointed recently. This is not acceptable and does not meet Premier Sales' quality policy so they are anxious to alert RPD to the consequences of any failure in quality control.
>
> Mr Pantos calls together his workers to explain the problem and the serious risk to the business if Premier Sales cancel their order. They review their QC (Quality Control) procedures and note the following problems:
>
> *Product identification and tracing*: Each batch of incoming fruit should be coded and the code then used in all production records to help them trace any problems back to the source. Some records were not being properly kept.
>
> *Process control*: Control over processing conditions (particularly pasteurization temperature and time, but also any delays in processing that would allow the fruit to darken) should be monitored and recorded. This was being done for processing conditions but not for other aspects of production which was likely to have caused colour variation.
>
> *Inspection and testing*: This should be carried out at all stages from the purchase of raw fruits to the final packing. Although this was being done at present for incoming fruit, there were no regular checks afterwards.
>
> The workers agreed with Mr Pantos that they should routinely ensure that the product is of good quality, not just occasionally, but every batch. If there are problems they should identify them so that they can be dealt with quickly, with minimum losses. The company had a quality plan, which employees had contributed to, so they are committed to it, but it clearly was not being used properly, as the letter from Premier Sales showed. Everyone must be clear about their responsibilities in the process and Mr Pantos would review the need for staff to have appropriate training so that they can carry out those responsibilities to maximum effect.

Figure 3.3   *Example of a case study information sheet*

Exercises (also known as 'Syndicate exercises' or 'Application exercises')
These techniques are used to build participants' confidence by undertaking activities and being allowed to make mistakes within the safe environment of the training course. They encourage learning by doing, and are used to gain experience of new techniques and processes. The exercises are split into three phases: an introduction of what is required (5 minutes), a supervised exercise in groups or four to five (30–180 minutes) and a review (20–30 minutes). It is useful to print the instructions for the exercise onto a handout, particularly if there are several phases or activities to be covered. These should explain what is required, how it is to be done, the time available and what should be reported back to the whole group (e.g. Figure 3.4). As each group works through the exercise the trainer should monitor their performance and correct any errors or

> **Calculation of process yield**
>
> *Using information from the previous exercise, complete the following calculations of the yield of product from raw materials using dried fruit as an example*
>
> | | |
> |---|---:|
> | Weight of fresh fruit | 100 kg |
> | Weight of peel, seeds, etc. (20%) | .... kg |
> | Weight of useful fruit | .... kg |
> | If fresh fruit costs USh200 per kg, what is the actual cost per kg of useful fruit? | .... USh |
> | Weight of fruit placed in drier | .... kg |
> | Water content of fruit is 85%, so weight of moisture in the fruit is: | .... kg |
> | Weight of solids in the fruit | .... kg |
> | After drying the solids do not change, but the water content is reduced to 15%: what is the total weight of solids after drying? | .... kg |

Figure 3.4 *Example of an instruction sheet for a group exercise*

misinterpretations without actually doing the exercise for the group. During the review, ask each group to report back on what they have achieved and what are the main lessons learned. The trainer should relate participants' findings to the context and objectives of the session and highlight what has been learned.

Instructional talks

Bearing in mind the comments at the start of this chapter regarding learning by doing, rather than by listening, keep instructional talks (or lectures) to a minimum. There are, however, occasions when a talk is a quick and straightforward method of providing information, particularly when it is illustrated using an overhead projector (OHP), slides or samples. An instructional talk should not usually exceed 20 minutes and should be used as a method for participants to learn a specific piece of information linked with other techniques in a session. There is a danger that less confident or inexperienced trainers will continue talking for much longer to retain control of the group.

Trainers should, therefore, be aware of including talks in session guides, particularly if these are to be used by other trainers. Where talks are included, the guide should be clear about the purpose of the talk and exactly what is to be covered.

When using an OHP to illustrate a talk the following points should be borne in mind:

○ switch it off when not directly in use to reduce noise and avoid distraction;
○ use prepared acetates which are likely to be more legible and better thought out than ones written during the session;
○ reveal one line at a time using an overlay to create more interest; give information step-by-step to add impact and control the pace of learning;
○ rest a pencil on the acetate to emphasize a particular subject, rather than attempting to point to it;
○ stand out of the way of participants' view of the screen;
○ remember that an OHP magnifies about 30 times – both the message and any mistakes!;

Visit to a food preparation area		
Examine each of the aspects below when visiting the unit and score each one (1 = poor, 10 = excellent). Comment on each aspect.		
	Score	Comment
1. Suitability of floor		
2. Ventilation		
3. Storage facilities		
4. Hygiene		
5. Refrigeration		
6. Evidence of infestation		
7. Preparation surfaces		
8. Lighting		
9. Waste disposal		
10. Water supplies		

Figure 3.5   *Example of an instructional visit sheet*

○ use pictures, drawings, colour and humour to increase the impact of the OHP;
○ keep the information simple and clear; and
○ as a general rule use a maximum of eight lines per acetate and six words per line.

Instructional visits

This technique is used to focus participants' attention on specific subjects of interest that they should look out for during a visit. It is a good way of maximizing the learning potential from a visit and putting previous learning into a practical or real-life situation. It also provides a framework for participants to ask questions during the visit. A common fault, when participants visit a factory, market, farm or other relevant place during a training course, is the lack of preparation beforehand. As a result they walk around the visit site without any clear understanding of what to look for or what to ask and hence learn less than is possible. Trainers should prepare for the visit by making a prior visit to the site and discussing with the owner or manager the purpose of the exercise and the areas they wish participants to visit. This is essential to enable workers at the site to be prepared for questions and comments from participants and to avoid potentially embarrassing situations arising from lack of communication about the visitors' intentions.

The technique has three phases: an introduction (5 minutes) in which the purpose is explained and a visit sheet (Figure 3.5) handed out; the visit itself, which can be anything from 15 minutes to half a day; and a discussion of what was found during the visit (30–60 minutes). Before the session, it is useful to prepare a matrix of participants' names and the questions on the visit sheet

Question/Topic	John	Gladys	Anil	Mario
1. Suitability of floor	2	3	2	4
2. Ventilation	1	5	2	5
3. Storage facilities	3	3	4	5
4. Hygiene	7	4	2	8
5. Refrigeration	4	7	6	5
6. Evidence of infestation	7	4	2	7
7. Preparation surfaces	5	6	3	5
8. Lighting	8	9	8	7
9. Waste disposal	7	2	3	6
10. Water supplies	6	5	5	7

Figure 3.6 *Matrix for analysing an instructional visit*

(Figure 3.6) and then on return from the visit, ask participants to write their scores for each question on the matrix. This then shows any differences in participants' perceptions of what they have seen and heard during the visit and provides a focus for subsequent discussions.

In the analysis of the matrix (Figure 3.6), the trainer could, for example, focus on apparent differences in perception of hygiene or waste disposal by Gladys and Anil compared to John and Mario and use this to focus the discussion of requirements and facilities.

Role play

In role plays, participants are asked to enact a role that they may have at work or in a similar situation. It is most beneficial when dealing with face-to-face situations such as a buyer/seller relationship, a manager/employee problem or a consultant/client discussion. The technique is suitable where real life situations, behavioural attitudes or more complex topics need to be discussed and participants can receive advice and constructive criticism within the safe environment of the training course. Normally a role play would last from 30 to 60 minutes although shorter sessions that specifically illustrate one topic are also useful. Trainers should prepare role plays carefully, to ensure that the objective and expected outcome are clearly defined and also the way in which the role play will contribute to the overall session is thought through. They should provide each participant with a clearly written brief of his or her role and other trainees should be given clear instructions of their part in analysing what happens during the role play. The trainer should ensure that all participants agree to a code whereby only constructive criticism of the actors or their behaviour is permitted in the review.

Food production sessions

The purposes of these sessions are as follows:

- to gain experience of the methods used to select and prepare raw materials, to process and pack products and to apply quality assurance/good manufacturing practice;
- to gain experience of organisational and scheduling aspects of food production;
- to undertake preliminary costing of production;
- to assess variability in the quality of foods; and
- to devise a preliminary marketing plan for selling the products that are produced.

Outline of the sessions

You will work in groups with one person as the manager who is responsible for all of the work that is done and for reporting the results of the production. Normally two hours will be allowed for processing, recording production data and cleaning the equipment and facilities (the time may vary depending on the products to be made). At the end of the production, all facilities and equipment should be cleaned and replaced in the store in preparation for the next day's production. The manager is expected to allocate the work required to each member of the group and to supervise that work during production. Particular care should be taken to ensure that all members of the group work in a way that is safe for themselves and other people in the food room. The manager is also responsible for ensuring that correct hygiene and food handling practices are always observed by the group. Before each session the managers are responsible for the following (agreed with the trainer):

- deciding the amount of food to be produced and planning the production process;
- deciding on the types and amounts of equipment and materials to be used and the costs;
- ensuring that all equipment and materials are in place for the session;
- determining the expected quality requirements for raw materials and finished products;
- planning the work of each member of the group; and
- marketing/selling strategy.

MANAGERS SHOULD PLAN THEIR REQUIREMENTS IN DISCUSSIONS WITH THEIR GROUP NO LATER THAN THE DAY BEFORE EACH PRODUCTION SESSION

During each session managers should supervise the work of the group and record all relevant production data.

After each session the manager should ensure that the financial records are completed and report back on the successes/failures of the production and how the product(s) are expected to be sold.

Notes for production managers

As a manager for the production session, please read these notes and organise a meeting of the production team *at least one day before the start of the session*. You will be given an order for a specified amount of product to be made during your production session. During the meeting you are responsible for planning the production and organising the work of the team in order that you can meet the requirements of the order. You should, therefore, ensure that everyone is clear about what they should do before, during and after the session.

You will need to organize the following aspects of production (do not forget to delegate some of these responsibilities):

1. Calculate the amounts and costs of ingredients and raw materials needed.
2. Decide what equipment you will need and calculate the cost of it.
3. Decide who will do what.
4. Ensure that all financial records will be completed.
5. Ensure that quality assurance records are completed.
6. Decide what the marketing/selling strategy will be for your product(s).

Figure 3.7 *Instruction sheet for a simulation exercise involving management of a food production unit*

Simulation exercises

These are simplified models of a real life situation where participants adopt roles that are similar to those in their jobs. The exercise is controlled by rules that are set out by the trainer with participants' agreement and are monitored by the trainer. These compress the time taken for an activity so that trends and behaviour become more obvious and relationships between cause and effect can be more clearly demonstrated. They can last from 20 to 30 minutes up to a full day (as described in the Uganda case study of practical food production. *See* Chapter 13). The simulation is followed by a review (30–40 minutes) in which feedback is given by participants and trainers on the events that took place in the simulation and the lessons to be learned. The technique is useful to show how real life systems operate, including management styles, good or poor exchange of information and planning for decision-making. New behaviour and skills can be tested out by participants within the controlled environment of the training course. An example of a simulation exercise is shown in Figure 3.7.

Games

Games are an effective, stimulating way of learning, for both literate and illiterate trainees. *The Marketing Game®* is one example of this approach. The game lasts for about two to three hours, during which time participants learn about different elements of marketing. The case study in Sudan (Chapter 12) uses this particular marketing game as part of the training course.

Techniques that are used to gain participants' commitment

Actions plans

Action plans are best used as a private exercise by each participant to relate what has been learned to their own individual situation. A prepared action plan is given to participants at the start of the course and the trainer encourages participants to fill in specific actions at each opportunity during the course where a new topic is introduced or discussed.

Summary technique

This is used to draw together ideas from a session and to enable participants to crystallize their thoughts and possible actions as a result of the session. The trainer identifies the key points from the session and summarizes them on the flipchart. This may be linked to action planning (above).

Trainers' guides

A sequence of the techniques described above should be used by trainers in a structured way to achieve the objectives of a particular session. This needs to be carefully planned in advance to ensure that each session runs smoothly. It is usual for trainers to prepare their own guide to use as an *aide-mémoire* during the sessions. This also helps to maintain good timekeeping and to prevent the trainer losing the focus of what is to be achieved. The first part of a typical trainers' guide is shown in Figure 3.8.

The purposes of trainers' guides are:

○ to outline the technical areas to be covered in the session (and by implication, those that are to be omitted);
○ to indicate the training method to be used at each stage;
○ to indicate the expected time required for each activity; and
○ to indicate the materials and equipment required for each session.

It is important to realize that trainers' guides are intended for use by the person who has written them. They are not a set of instructions, but a guide to how a session can be run. They should, therefore, be modified by a second trainer before they are used, both to ensure that the trainer is clear about what is to be done, feels comfortable with the methods to be used and has ownership of the materials. Passing trainers' guides to other trainers does not work if they are inexperienced and lack the confidence to modify

> **DAY 5**
> **Session 2**
>
> **Food legislation**
>
> **Learning objectives**
> By the end of this session, the participants will:
>
> o know the main points of the food laws in the country;
> o know how to find information about the laws that relate to their own products.
>
> **Resources required**
> o flipchart and pens;
> o samples of foods and food labels;
> o overheads OHP5/2–1 – OHP5/2–6;
> o handouts HO5/2–1 – HO5/2–4.
>
> **Duration** 120 minutes
>
> **Sequence of activities**
> o buzz group;
> o exercise;
> o discussion;
> o review.
>
> *Trainer's notes*
> Before the start of the session, ensure that sample products and packaging for the products to be included are available. Write the objectives on the flipchart.
>
> 1. Introduction
>   Explain the purposes of the session as follows: by being aware of the regulations under which foods are made and sold, participants can meet individual product standards more easily and, therefore, ensure that their products have an acceptable quality and the company avoids prosecution. A second competent to this session is how participants can find out about individual legal standards for their own products.
>   Ask participants if they have any other objectives and write these on the flipchart.
> 2. Buzz group (20–30 minutes)
>   Write on the flipchart 'What laws apply to foods?' and ask participants to work in groups of four for 10 minutes to answer the question. Review their answers and draw out the main points.

Figure 3.8   *Example of the first part of a trainers' guide*

the guides to suit their own style of training. Instead they attempt to follow the guide as it is written and often fail to achieve a 'flow' in the session, constantly stopping to check whether they have followed the guide correctly. The session becomes interrupted and the delivery, instead of appearing relaxed, seems stilted and out of touch with the participants.

Putting failures right

Even experienced participative trainers make mistakes and Table 3.2 shows some of

	Mistake	Likely cause	Possible solution
Preparation	Not sure what has been achieved, session unfocused. Participants 'get lost'.	Lack of clearly stated outcomes. Lack of preparation, unclear learning objectives, over-estimate of participants' abilities.	Prepare the session by thinking through precisely what participants should do, when and for how long. Divide session into small units or activities and time them realistically. Allow time to obtain feedback from participants to ensure that they understand the topic so far.
Introduction	Participants did not understand the purpose of the session or what was expected of them. They showed reluctance or lack of interest in taking part.	Trainer failed to introduce the session clearly or to 'sell' the required activity by gaining participants' agreement.	Introduce the session by placing it into context with previous/later sessions and clearly show what it is that participants are expected to achieve and do during the session. Check before the session that the intended activities are suitable for participants (particularly if the activities impinge on religious, gender or dietary considerations).
Practice	Participants made many errors during exercises or practical work, did not learn to do tasks properly, or their concentration lapsed.	Trainer gave poor demonstrations, missed out important points, strayed away from the main topic or failed to hold participants' attention.	Do not rush demonstrations; repeat them (several times) if necessary until all participants understand the technique. Prepare most carefully so that a relatively few important points are emphasized several times. Check participants' understanding of key points as the session progresses. Answer all questions but return to the main subject as soon as possible and inform participants that this is what you are doing. Do not overload participants with too much information. Break learning stages into smaller units if participants find the topic difficult.
Participants not learning	Trainer spends too much time talking, lacks confidence, or took over from participants when something went wrong. Participants give up or get stuck over a problem.	Trainer talking too much or not allowing participants to make mistakes in a controlled environment. Trainer fails to correct errors or mistakes when they are made and fails to find causes of the errors before correcting them (applies particularly to issues of participant safety).	Set time aside for participants to practise and make mistakes under supervision, ensure that participants are actively working for at least 75 per cent of the session time. Keep participants informed of their progress and highlight successes. Find the basic causes of errors and discuss these with participants so that they can put these right themselves before moving onto the next activity or next practice session.
Trainer's manner	Participants' interest and/or confidence declined during the session or they show lack of co-operation and irritation with the trainer – possibly even resentment and complaints.	Trainer is not interested in the session, or in the participants, lacks confidence in the activity or in the way it is being taught. Trainer is condescending and 'talks down' to participants or finds personal fault with one or more of them.	Trainers should examine their motivation and attitude and avoid/change the training if they do not enjoy the activities. They should not undertake an activity unless completely familiar with it. They should regard each participant as a mature individual who is there because they want to learn, and approach them positively with a view to encouraging their progress. If criticism seems necessary, first ask what fault the trainer may have to contribute to the situation.

Table 3.2 *Examples of some common failings in participative training and possible solutions*

the more common ones with possible causes and ways of improving performance.

Practical training sessions

While increased theoretical, technical and business knowledge are important components of training, it should be remembered that the final goal for the participants is its application to the profitable production of safer, improved, processed foods that have a greater market potential. Practical production sessions in which participants apply new knowledge and learn by doing are thus an essential element of any course.

Most practical skills, such as the use of equipment, production routines for specific food products, quality control techniques and good hygiene can be learned in short practical sessions. However, for processing that has a large component of craft skill, such as bakery and confectionery, the techniques can only be learned after extended practice. Short practical training is, however, useful to provide participants with the basic techniques, skills and confidence that they can build on with time.

The provision of practical training is generally, in terms of organization, the greatest challenge facing trainers. In most developing countries there are few dedicated facilities with the required equipment, and trainers have to use facilities that are often far from ideal. In these situations, a great deal of imagination and flexibility is required to provide adequate sessions. There is a danger that the use of inadequate facilities can give the wrong signals to participants. In such cases trainers should use any shortcomings, related for example to hygiene, safety or ventilation, so that participants critically identify faults and develop a plan of action to remedy them.

Practical training sessions provide the opportunity for participants to both make mistakes in food production within a controlled environment and to learn how to collaborate in teamwork and management. The sessions should not be viewed as simply allowing participants to follow a detailed set of instructions but should be regarded as the opportunity for them to apply their experience and the knowledge gained in theoretical sessions. For example, participants may have learnt about the use of food preservatives and their allowable limits in parts per million. In practical work they apply this knowledge by calculating the amount of preservative required in batches of different sizes. Through repetition over several days they become comfortable with the calculations and are able to use them in their own enterprises.

When organized as production sessions, in which one participant acts as the 'manager of the day' and delegates tasks to their team, practical training can also be used to highlight methods of work organization and management style that are difficult to teach by other means. This approach is described in the previous section 'Putting failures right' and in the Uganda case study (Chapter 13).

The first step when planning any

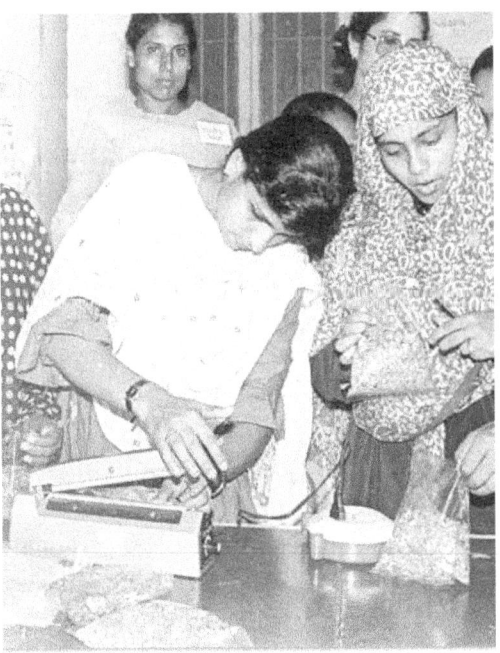

Practical sessions include modules on each part of the process, including packaging (IT/Farhad Hossain)

Class discussions at the end of practical sessions can help to identify and rectify problems (Midway Technology)

practical training is to carry out a training needs assessment as described in Chapter 2. The practical sessions can then be designed to meet the specific training needs identified. The trainer must have a clear understanding of the overall aims and objectives of the programme and how practical sessions can be used to meet these.

The way that theoretical aspects of food processing are linked to practical work requires careful planning. There are two broad ways that trainers approach this problem. The simplest approach is to provide all basic theory prior to commencing practical work and to add specific theory during the practical training as problems and issues dictate. Some trainers, however, prefer to introduce theory during the practical work.

Aims and objectives of practical training

Correctly designed practical training should integrate all skills and knowledge to successfully produce a food, manage a small business or practise correct food storage. It provides participants with the opportunity to:

o apply theoretical knowledge to food production;
o learn by doing;
o gain confidence through repetition;
o relate and apply knowledge gained to their own enterprise; and
o apply business management and costing skills to production.

It is very important for trainers to recognize that practical training sessions should also include business aspects that are relevant to production. Many participants find product costing calculations that involve yields, fuel costs, labour and equipment depreciation costs difficult to apply. Similarly, quality control checks, and in particular, the identification of critical control points in a production process where such tests should be applied, are often difficult concepts. The application and repetition of such calculations in an actual production session allows participants to gain confidence with using these concepts routinely. In this way they are more likely to apply them to their own enterprises.

The processing area

The room used for practical training requires careful selection and should be appropriate to the needs and circumstances of the participants. It would, for example, be inappropriate to train poor people with no access to electricity in the use of powered equipment. Not only would they not be able to apply what they had learnt but worse, they would probably believe that production is impossible without such resources. Similarly the appearance of the processing room should be similar to a room that they could build for themselves, while conforming to good manufacturing practice. A room that is full of tiled surfaces and stainless steel is likely to make participants think that food processing is not affordable by them. The following sections describe facilities for providing training to participants from small enterprises who in the main, have access to power and potable water.

In most cases, participants will work in groups which consist of no more than five people. The room must therefore be large enough to accommodate work tables for the required number of groups. Typically 16 participants, working in four groups require a room 8m by 10m. The room should not be overcrowded as safety must be a prime consideration. Adequate space is essential to allow movement by participants without the risk of accidents, particularly when carrying hot foods.

The layout of the processing room should demonstrate good manufacturing practice. It should allow the correct flow of materials around the room during production so that soiled incoming raw materials and packaging never cross with semi-finished or finished foods. Participants should wash their hands at the start of the day and after using the toilet or handling dirty materials. Rings, ties and jewellery should be removed. If available safe food-handling posters (Figure 3.9) should be displayed in the room.

Each group requires a large work table which ideally should be covered in 'melamine', aluminium sheet or stainless steel for good hygienic practice. An acceptable alternative is to cover the tables with a double layer of heavy-gauge polythene sheet which can be washed down at the end of each day. Table legs should be stood in cans containing kerosene, or water containing a few drops of detergent to prevent ants which can pose a major problem, particularly with sweet foods.

The practical room should be near to a classroom or seminar room. It should have a secure storage space for equipment and materials when they are not being used. Ideally the room should be on the ground floor for easy drainage when the floors are washed down. It should have a panelled ceiling, to avoid dust falling into products, have a washable concrete floor and double doors to allow easy access for equipment. The walls should be washable but not necessarily tiled. Good ventilation using ceiling fans, is important as in many cases considerable heat is generated during processing. Windows and doors should be fitted with insect-proof mesh. Finally, good lighting is required. If

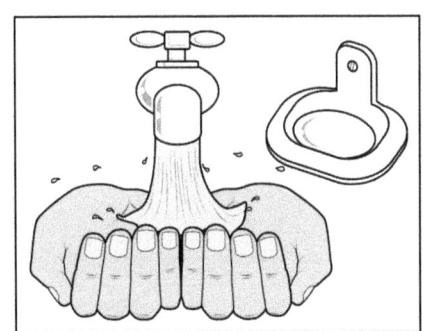

Make sure that anyone who will touch food always washes their hands properly using soap and clean water.

Cover all unpackaged food before it is sold. Stop insects, birds and animals from eating it first.

Take extra care over hygiene when preparing dairy, meat or fish products. They can cause dangerous food poisoning if special attention is not given to hygiene.

Figure 3.9 *Examples of posters to promote safe handling of foods*

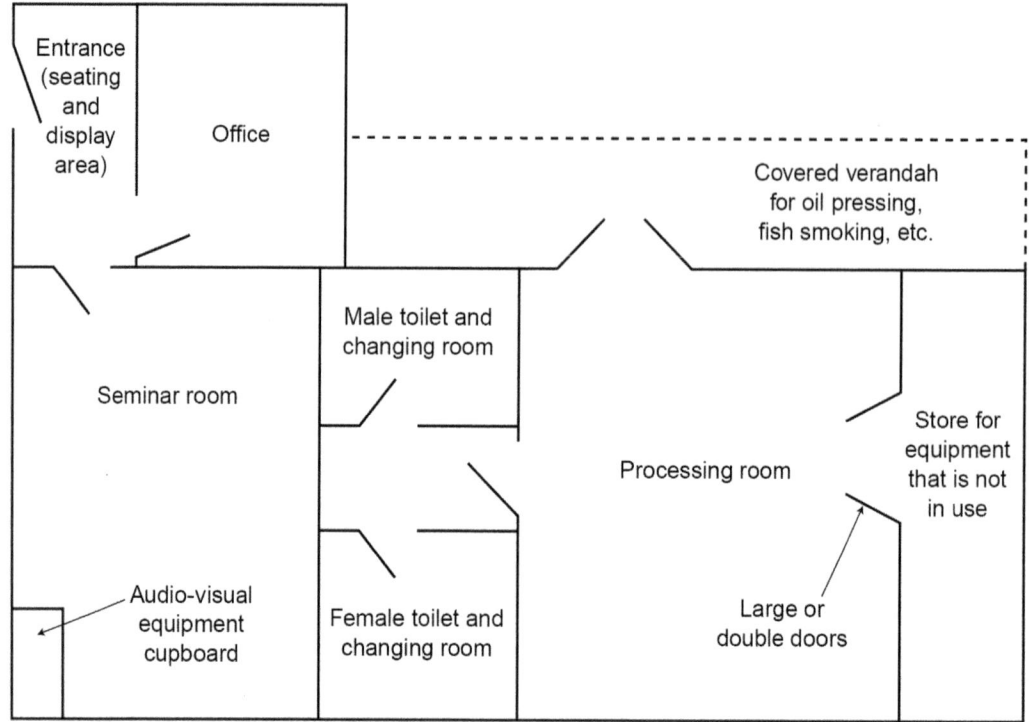

Figure 3.10 *Layout of a purpose-built training facility for food processing*

moving machinery is used, lighting should not solely consist of fluorescent tubes which can make a moving part appear stationary. A first aid box and fire extinguisher should be readily available in the training room in case of accidents. Figure 3.10 shows a typical layout for a practical training room.

All these considerations aim to demonstrate good practice which participants should aim to adopt, but at the same time not make them think that the facilities are unaffordable and not appropriate to them.

Toilets and changing rooms should be nearby but must not open directly onto the processing area. Protective coats and hats should be provided. Gloves may be needed to carry hot pots and pans or if fruit, particularly pineapple and papaya, is handled for long periods.

Depending on the type of processing, six double 13-amp electric sockets are required together with a good supply of drinking water. Ideally the water supply should be via taps over a large sink but hosepipes can be acceptable. If gas is to be used, all appliances should be checked by a competent technician prior to use and good ventilation is essential. When training people without access to electricity, heating by wood or charcoal is appropriate.

It is often useful to have a covered area outside, where for example, dirty incoming fruits and vegetables can be washed or bottles can be cleaned to avoid the danger of broken glass in the processing room. Any processes that involve burning wood, for example fish smoking, can also take place in this area. An area of the processing room should also be kept clear for the trainer to use a flipchart and other training materials.

The use of commercial facilities

In some circumstances it may be preferable to use production facilities within an existing enterprise for practical training. The use of dairies in the Peruvian and Ugandan case studies (Chapters 9 and 13) and bakeries in

Participants learn about cheese production in a commercial dairy in Uganda (Midway Technology)

the Bangladesh case study (see Chapter 5) are examples of this approach.

The use of commercial facilities for practical training has a number of potential advantages and disadvantages for both participants and trainers:

Advantages: For training courses that are intended to enable participants to establish or improve a food processing enterprise, the most realistic training environment is a processing plant that is already established and operating at a high standard. It provides a model for participants to copy and enables real-life problems to be addressed within a working environment that is difficult to fully simulate in a training room. For example, topics that can be dealt with in an integrated way in a commercial environment include fixed and variable costs, plant layout, staffing levels, management methods and production and quality control methods. All of this information is more readily available within the factory, and the environment itself will often generate useful and thought-provoking debate. It is difficult to integrate these topics so well in a training room, even when simulation exercises are used and adequate equipment is provided.

Limitations and constraints: There are a number of important constraints and potential disadvantages that should be taken into account before using commercial food processing plant for training; not least the prospect of trainees increasing competition for the manufacturer who has assisted the training programme. When a business faces the normal daily pressures of producing foods at a high quality for profit, the additional burden of having a number of eager participants on site, who are all inexperienced but wishing to learn, can cause problems.

The commitment of owners or managers of commercial facilities towards allowing their plant to be used for training can be enhanced by hiring support personnel from the company and using them as trainers and facilitators during training sessions. This not only increases their self-confidence and feeling of worth in their work, but may also increase their knowledge and skills, which in turn benefits the host company. The trainer should discuss in advance with the senior management of the factory the scope of the proposed activities and any areas that may cause difficulty. Only when both parties are confident that their problems can be addressed and their needs met, should arrangements be made to conduct training on the premises.

The logistics of the training exercise must be carefully considered and planned in advance. For example, the owners may have areas of the factory that they do not wish

In many countries training is carried out in commercial bakeries (IT/Mike Battcock)

participants to enter, they may be concerned that product contamination may occur, substandard products will be produced by trainees or that routine work by their staff will be adversely affected, leading to a reduction in output and lower income. Each of these concerns should be addressed during the planning discussions between the trainer and owner or manager. Additionally, duplicate equipment may be necessary to allow all groups to undertake production work, preparation or monitoring activities. Hand washing and toilet facilities must be examined and decisions made as to their suitability, and the space available for group discussion and reviews should be noted. A written agreement on the use of the facilities with the company's directors must be obtained and any fees for use should be negotiated and agreed in advance with final payment at the end of the programme.

A commercial company may wish to avoid training competitors who may attend courses simply to gain an insight into specific operational practices. Additionally, the company may require restricted access to participants who operate in their sales area. These may take the form of scrutiny at the participant selection stage or a formal agreement to be signed by participants agreeing not to operate within a given distance from the site.

Over-use of materials such as cleaning agents, packaging materials and ingredients may occur through participants' inexperience. The trainer should discuss the potential costs with the factory owner when planning the session and ensure that additional materials costs are included in the budget for the training course. Participants should be provided with a materials budget to encourage control of their use. During reviews of production sessions, discussions should include yield and variance analysis of all costs to identify good and bad practice and encourage optimum use of resources.

Equipment required for practical training

As far as possible the equipment used for practical training should be selected from what is locally available and the number of imported items should be kept to a minimum. There is little point in training people how to produce a food item if, in reality it is impossible for them to access the equipment that is used. In the past some training programmes have involved importing a custom-built trailer full of expensive stainless steel equipment. This has a negative impact, as participants may not consider locally available alternatives and, worse, they may come to believe that it would be impossible to start production without such imported equipment.

The trainer has a key role in advising on locally available equipment and should have a knowledge of local suppliers and manufacturers, plus catalogues to advise participants on suitable alternatives. The choice of equipment should be related to the type of participants being trained and their individual circumstances. If owners of medium-scale enterprises have the financial resources to import, more sophisticated production systems would be appropriate. The trainer should decide on a scale of equipment that is appropriate for the participants by asking them about the size of their businesses during the training needs assessment.

It is clearly impossible to list the equipment required to provide practical training as so much will depend on the local circumstances. An example of the equipment needed to provide bakery training for 16 small scale urban bakers in Kampala, Uganda is shown in Figure 3.11.

3 household-sized electric or gas ovens
4 sets of scales (0 to 10kg)
4 sets of scales (0 to 500g)
4 mixing bowls
8 each of wooden spoons, spatulas, knives, chopping boards
32 bread tins, cake tins
4 pastry cutters
4 electric dough mixers
1 liquidizer
4 flour sieves

Figure 3.11 *Equipment requirements for practical bakery training*

Planning production sessions

Practical training offers a great challenge to trainers. Many things can go wrong including power or water failures, equipment breakdown and batches of food that, due to an error, turn out disastrously wrong. The trainer should avoid any frustration in such circumstances and use failures to illustrate some of the real life difficulties of commercial food processing and use participants' own experience of ways in which the difficulties can be overcome.

Good planning prior to the course will give the trainer maximum control over the practical work and minimize foreseeable problems. Remember: *failing to plan is planning to fail*. The trainer should plan using three time-scales for practical production sessions.

Things to plan at least four weeks ahead:

o Ensure that the training room is available and that all services are working.

o Ensure that all equipment is available and operational and/or steps are being taken to purchase, repair or construct it.
o Prepare all audio-visual materials and file them ready for use.
o Prepare all training notes and foods such as wines and fermented pickles that need time to make on the course.
o Make sure that all foods, ingredients and packaging materials are ordered.

Plan one week ahead for the following:

o If technical assistants or resource persons are to be used, make sure they are fully briefed on how to operate equipment safely and where all materials are stored.
o If examples of spoilt foods are to be used, prepare samples.

Plan one or two days ahead:

o Advise technical assistants of foods and equipment to be prepared.
o If group production managers are to be used, discuss their requirements and make sure everything is ordered.
o Make sure they have planned the sessions with their teams.

Implementation of practical training

The methodology and style of delivery of practical training varies with the ability and personality of individual trainers and the needs, educational standards and perspectives of the participants. No one method can be universal but three main approaches can be seen in the case studies.

In the first approach, described in the Peruvian case study (see Chapter 9), the trainer demonstrates and explains each step of the production process and the participants then work in groups or individually to repeat what they have observed. The trainer and assistants move from group to group providing guidance as required. This approach, essentially 'doing by copying', is particularly suited to training people with low levels of literacy and numeracy.

The second approach is for the trainer to provide detailed written instruction sheets to describe the processing methods which the participants then follow. Clearly only applicable to literate participants, the method has the disadvantage of not enabling participants to think for themselves and resolve problems. In essence the trainer has done all the work for them.

The third approach, as illustrated in the Ugandan and UNIDO case studies (see Chapters 13 and 14), simulates the operation of a small processing enterprise. This involves the selection of a production manager each day for each team of participants. The manager supervises the team to produce foods that have a specified quality for a pre-set price, based on an order provided by the trainer.

Whatever approach is used, time should be allowed for a review at the end of the practical session for participants to analyse the day's work. This should be structured to allow all participants to contribute. It is the most valuable part of practical training because it enables participants to put theoretical learning and their own experience into context, to exchange experiences with each other and to examine benefits and problems of working in a team. The review also provides valuable feedback to the trainer, pointing to areas which need to be reinforced or changes that should be considered to the course. In every group of participants there will be one or two individuals who are leaders and if not properly controlled may dominate others. The trainer must control these individuals both in practical sessions and reviews to allow all to express their opinions.

Modifying training sessions for use in a commercial facility

The working arrangements of a commercial plant are often dictated by the arrival of the raw material for processing. If, for example, the material is on site at 8 a.m., then training sessions that involve production should be scheduled to begin at that time to prevent deterioration of the material. The length of the working day is normally a minimum eight hours and if participants are expected to be working for the whole day, this should be negotiated with them prior to their attendance.

Scheduling groups to work on different pieces of equipment, different raw materials and packaging, all demand forward planning. Normally this is initially undertaken by the course tutor to ensure the feasibility of moving participants around the factory without any undue disruption to production routines. Similarly, the capacity of equipment must be examined before finalising production sessions. This is both in relation to the cost of a batch of product, when materials costs are being met by the training course, and the time required to prepare raw materials and clean down after production.

The location of equipment and materials stores may cause confusion during busy production sessions and a simple plan of the plant is useful to indicate where goods and equipment may be found. Alternatively a visit to the site by participants for familiarization purposes prior to production can be undertaken.

The steps required to implement training in a commercial facility are as follows:

1. Document the programme and participants' needs.
2. List the key points required at the site for training.
3. Visit a number of potential sites.
4. Involve the factory management in discussions.
5. Select an appropriate site and agree the terms for hire.
6. Agree any limitations to use of the site.
7. Confirm in writing terms and conditions.
8. Note the provision of space, equipment, water, electricity, production area and layout, toilets, canteen, preparation facilities, production facilities, monitoring facilities, packaging facilities, materials.
9. If necessary, note the cost and availability of local accommodation and make arrangements for meals and travel to and from the site.
10. Make arrangements to ensure the availability of factory personnel to assist as

resource persons/trainers in the production plant.

When the initial planning phase is complete, the factory staff will have a clear understanding of the programme needs and the trainer has a picture of the benefits and constraints of the site. The trainer can then construct a production schedule in line with the factory product range, containing estimated usage of materials, equipment and factory space. After agreeing this with the factory staff, the trainer then selects teams of participants containing a balance of technical, commercial and management expertise. A maximum team size of five should be set to enable all members to play an active role and gain experience of managing the team.

Delivering training in commercial facilities
Few if any factories have specific training facilities and, like production activities, the trainer should organize a clear training plan within these limitations. Clear instructions to the teams of participants are required. Safety aspects of equipment or material handling should be emphasized and the responsibility placed with nominated team managers to ensure compliance. Teams are given quality assurance, production control and costing record sheets which, when completed, are used in feedback discussions.

Safety of participants and damage liability
A simple set of 'do's and don'ts' should be planned and the trainer should make sure that all participants are fully aware of them before starting any practical work. Appropriate clothing and footwear should be worn to prevent slipping or damage to clothes from spillage. The dangers associated with specific pieces of equipment, including cutters, slicers and pressure cookers, must be explained to participants and rules about their use should be agreed in advance. Liability for accidents in a commercial facility must be clarified with the factory owners and the action to be taken as a result of an accident agreed. A simple first aid box should be mandatory and its contents checked before production sessions proceed.

If the commercial facility is leased to the training organization, liability for damage resides with the latter. All participants are normally careful when using equipment, but incorrect assembly, wrong temperatures of use or incorrect cleaning materials may damage machinery or the factory environment. Potential problems should be discussed with the owner before training begins and participants should be made aware of the likelihood of causing damage. The trainer should carefully monitor participants' activities and take all reasonable precautions to prevent damage occurring.

4
Monitoring, evaluation and follow-up

It is useful to carry out monitoring immediately after the course in order to identify the particular needs, provide technical assistance and improve the training.

Carmen Rodriguez, Peru

Introduction

Monitoring, evaluation and impact assessment are three exercises which should feature in every training programme. They should be taken seriously by the organizers of training and sufficient time should be allocated to the collection of relevant monitoring data. People may see these exercises as pointless and time consuming, but if this attitude is taken, the training itself will most likely lose its point and become a waste of time for both organizers and participants.

Monitoring and impact assessment complement each other. Monitoring provides the information necessary for day-to-day decision-making and also provides baseline data for the impact assessment. Evaluation at the end of a course allows the trainer to assess the effectiveness of the training. Together, monitoring, evaluation and impact assessment are invaluable in determining the effectiveness of the course and measuring the impact of the training on the recipients or beneficiaries.

Monitoring progress versus impact assessment

Monitoring progress is the routine collection, analysis and use of information about how suitable the training course is for the participants.

Regular monitoring of training courses enables the organizers to:

○ make decisions on how to improve the course;
○ decide what effect the course is having on the participants;
○ ensure that the course is accountable to all those who are interested in it. For example, beneficiaries, clients, staff, donors and management.

Evaluation is carried out by obtaining the participants' views at the end of a course and by analysis of the data collected during monitoring. Evaluation of a course ensures that:

○ it is suitable for the intended participants and responds to their individual needs; and
○ the content and style of teaching are fully understood by the participants.

Impact assessment is a periodic assessment of the effectiveness of the training some time after the training has finished (e.g. after six months).

An assessment of the impact of the course enables the organizers to:

○ measure the progress towards meeting the overall objectives;
○ make decisions about the future direction of the course; and
○ determine the cost-effectiveness of the particular course.

How to determine the effectiveness of the training course

The *effectiveness* of a training course is a measure of how well the training met the expectations of the participants and how useful it has been to them in their work. To determine the effectiveness of training, there are several key points to monitor:

○ Does the training meet the needs of the participants?

- Is it held at convenient locations and times?
- Are the training skills applied to the field situation, i.e. are the trainees passing on their skills?
- Do participants feel the training is useful or helpful?
- What suggestions do the participants have for improvement of the course?

Monitoring of the training course

Ideally, monitoring should be carried out at the end of daily sessions and also at the end of the course. To observe the more long-term effects, monitoring of participants should continue after they have completed the training.

Monitoring of individual sessions

At the beginning of courses, trainers should have a plan for what they hope to achieve at the end of each day. This plan should not so much reflect the number of items they hope to talk about, but rather the number of things they hope the participants will have learnt by the end of the session or day. It is important that trainers take time at the end of the day to assess how much the participants have learnt. It is pointless for trainers to continue imparting information if it is not understood by the participants. Good trainers will listen to the opinions of the participants and will adjust the pace, style and content of training to suit the individuals.

It is useful to get feedback from the participants immediately after a particular session has finished, as their opinions are still fresh in their minds. If they have encountered any major problems, it may be possible to include an extra session to clarify issues. The feedback can take a number of different forms. It may be a written questionnaire or examination. Alternatively, it could be an informal group discussion or a more formal presentation and question and answer session. In the Uganda case study (see Chapter 13), the approach is to carry out ongoing monitoring of each day's training. The participants are given evaluation forms for each session which they fill in upon completion of the respective course components (see Figure 4.1). They also take part in regular group discussions. The trainer is able to measure the degree of learning which is taking place and can modify or reinforce problem areas as the course progresses. The monitoring is reinforced in practical sessions by peer review in which group members report on the manager's performance and the managers report on the group or individual performances. A different approach is taken in the Bangladesh case study (Chapter 5). At the end of each day's training, two participants are asked to make a presentation to the rest of the group on what they perceive to be the most important learning points of the day. A question and answer session follows this where any misunderstandings can be clarified. Not only does this approach highlight problem areas, it ensures that all participants concentrate on the day's activities, since they may be selected to give the feedback.

Evaluation at the end of the course

At the end of the course it is useful to receive feedback on how useful the participants found the whole course. In addition to questions regarding course content and the level and style of training, it is useful to find out the participants' views on the timing and location of the course. It should be remembered that it is not always simple to monitor the effectiveness of the training programme. Evaluations carried out immediately after the course are often not a true reflection of the usefulness of the course for a number of reasons:

- the participants may have enjoyed the opportunity to attend and to meet new people and this clouds their perception of the usefulness;
- they may have found some of the sessions difficult and confuse 'ease of understanding' with 'usefulness'; and
- if asked to report back to the course organizer, they may feel an obligation to be complimentary about the course.

SESSION EVALUATION: SUMMARY SHEET

Session Title: Electrical safety
Date: 20 October 1996
Presenter(s): Mr. B. Buga

1. The material presented was:	2. The pace was:		3. I learnt:	
Extremely Interesting 20%	Much too fast		A great deal	40%
Interesting 80%	A little too fast		Some	60%
Somewhat interesting	Just right	60%	Not very much	
Not interesting	A little too slow	40%	Nothing	
Boring	Much too slow			

4. The organization of the session was:		5. What I learnt was:		6. Generally the session was:	
Extremely well done	20%	Very important	60%	Excellent	20%
Well done	20%	Important	20%	Good	20%
Satisfactory	60%	Not very important	20%	Satisfactory	40%
Poorly done		Useless		Fair	20%
Very badly done				Poor	

7. Please write at least one specific comment here:

Very important information concerning electrical safety to minimize accidents; Charts for safety should always be displayed to ensure adherence; Whoever deals with any electrical appliance or electricity in general has to be satisfactorily aware of the consequences; I learnt that wires must be connected tightly and distribution be carried out in a proper and standard way; It is important that all electrically conducting equipment must be earthed properly.

Figure 4.1 Example of a summary of feedback by participants

Another method of evaluation is to carry out exercises with the course participants at the start of the course to determine the extent of their knowledge. This may be a short, written exercise or could be a problem-solving exercise. The same exercise is then carried out after completion of the course to determine how the participant's knowledge has improved. This approach is taken in the case studies from Bangladesh and Sudan (see Chapters 5 and 12). Subsequent training courses in these two countries are then modified according to the outcome of this exercise. In the South African case study (Chapter 10), a similar approach is adopted. At the beginning of the course the participants list their hopes and fears about the course on cards. These cards are referred to after the course is completed to ascertain whether their fears were allayed and their hopes and needs accommodated.

Some organizations may feel that they are not adequately equipped to implement a monitoring programme to measure the progress of their field workers. To help overcome these fears, the case study in Sudan has adopted a novel approach: at the same time that field workers are trained, members from the sending organization observe what the trainees are learning and are instructed on how to monitor their progress. After the monitoring information has been collected, it can be used to assess the impact of the training.

Assessment of the impact of training

In its simplest form, impact assessment can be described as identifying and measuring the significant changes which occur as a result of training, and gauging the degree to which they are sustainable. The impact of training can be assessed by visiting the participants in their working environment about

Discussion with participants at the end of a course provides invaluable feedback information (IT/Mike Battcock)

six months after the course. This gives a good opportunity to discuss the problems they are encountering and how they deal with them and to observe which of the training skills are being used.

How to assess the impact of training

After participating in a training course, trainees return to their respective workplaces to put the new-found skills into practice. It is important to measure how useful the training course was and whether the skills can easily be put into practice and to determine whether they need any further clarification or support.

Before assessing the impact of training, it is essential to be clear about the objectives. The objectives must be established and defined when the training is developed but it is possible that, as the training programme evolves, the objectives also change. This is perfectly acceptable as long as the reasons for change are justified.

Objectives are usually defined according to different time-scales and they may be split into the ultimate or overall, long-term, medium-term and short-term objectives. In the case study from Bangladesh (Chapter 5), the long-term objectives are to improve the standard of living of groups of landless women while the short-term objectives are to set up and implement training courses. In this particular example, training is only one element of a larger development programme designed to improve the livelihoods of poor people. In the Uganda case study (Chapter 13), the overall objectives of the training course are to provide business and technical support to the food processing sector by assisting entrepreneurs to develop existing or potential new businesses.

Once the objectives are established, the progress towards meeting them is measured. It is helpful if there are targets set which lead to the objective. These targets should then have indicators which are measurable and which give an indication of the progress towards the objective.

It is relatively easy to measure the progress towards meeting short-term objectives.

The ability to send children to school can be used as a proxy indicator of improved livelihoods (IT/Mike Lidbetter)

For example, if the objective is to carry out four training courses per year, it is very simple to monitor whether this has been achieved. Likewise, measuring an increase in income as a result of training is also fairly simple if baseline information is collected before the training. However, collecting accurate information on income levels is a sensitive issue and the answers may not always be a true reflection of the real situation.

Measuring the progress towards meeting objectives becomes more difficult when assessing qualitative information, as it involves a degree of personal judgement. It is, for example, difficult to measure an improvement in livelihood as this is a subjective issue. This type of information is usually collected by developing indicators which correspond to change. Also, the change in livelihood might be measured by an improvement in the standard of the individual's home, replacing a thatch with an iron roof, for instance. Another reliable indicator might be that the family have purchased more land or livestock or other consumer goods, such as electrical items. The fact that children are attending school is also a positive indicator that there has been an improvement in livelihoods.

Following the training described in the Bangladesh case study (Chapter 5), numerous families have witnessed changes in their lives. One family doubled the size of their home, both to accommodate the growing business but also to allow more living space for the family. More families are sending their children to school. There is extra money available to purchase medicines and medical treatment and for additional food for the family. All these factors are indicators of a positive change in people's lives.

Collecting the information

Once the objectives have been defined and suitable indicators chosen, a decision is made on the best tools to collect the relevant information. Inevitably, most of the methods involve talking to the people involved and finding their views.

A range of methodological tools are available, depending upon the circumstances and upon the type of information to be collected. For example, structured interviews or formal surveys are useful for collecting large amounts of quantitative data. These types of interviews do not allow for any deviation from the pre-defined questionnaire, but will generate vast amounts of quantifiable data. To probe more deeply and to follow up on issues which arise in the formal questionnaire, a more informal type of interview is required to compile a case history. This can be carried out with the aid of a checklist to ensure that all the relevant information is collected. It is possible to combine a formal and informal survey to collect both quantitative and qualitative information.

It is essential that the tools for collecting information – either the questionnaire or the checklist or the informal exercises – are field tested on a small sub-sample before embarking on the main group. If enumerators or interviewers are used to collect the information, they should be trained beforehand. It is essential that all persons collecting information are clear about the objectives of the exercise, that they understand the questions and approaches to be adopted and that data collection is carried out in a consistent manner across the sample. For the more participative exercises, it is essential that the interviewers are trained and experienced in the methods used.

The course participants are a valuable source of knowledge. They have attended the training course and have returned to the field to put their skills and knowledge into practice. Only they can reliably report on the suitability of the training course, the problems they have encountered and the recommendations they have for improving the course. Their opinions are vital.

In addition to checklists of key topics, an informal interview involves a greater degree of participation through exercises and games designed to answer the main questions. Scoring and ranking exercises help to interpret how useful the participants have found the training. They also help to define which are the most important constraints faced by the trainees. These exercises allow the interviewer to collect a wealth of information and to understand the context. They should only be used where they generate useful information, as they are very time-consuming and require the skills of a trained interviewer. Analysis of this type of information is more difficult than with the formal questionnaire approach, but is still invaluable in gaining a comprehensive understanding of the value of training.

Collecting baseline information before the start of training is very useful as it serves as a reference point against which progress can be measured. For example, collection of details of participants' knowledge of the subject, their income levels, the turnover of their business and the living conditions of themselves and their families are all useful indicators which can be re-collected at intervals after the training has been completed.

The best time to assess impact of a project
This depends to a large extent on the reason behind the assessment. If the assessment is to measure the overall success of the training in meeting its objectives, then periodic assessments, at one or two yearly intervals are the most useful. If the assessment is carried out too early in the life of the project, it may be difficult to determine whether any real impact has been made. Impact assessments carried out after one year to eighteen months are useful in shaping the future direction of the course.

If the assessment is concerned with the suitability of the individual training course, with a view to improving the next one, it is essential to carry out regular monitoring during and immediately after completion of the course.

Evaluation and assessment of the training course can be carried out either internally or externally. The organizers can choose to evaluate the project themselves; however, extra credibility is added if the evaluation is carried out by external people.

Evaluation should be viewed as a positive component of the training course. If the course has been successful in meeting its objectives, this will be highlighted by the evaluation. Similarly, any shortcomings in the course will also be highlighted. While the course organizers may not relish the thought of discovering that the course is not up to their expectations, constructive criticism is to the advantage of the organizers and the participants.

Cost-effective analysis
One of the objectives of the evaluation may be to measure the cost-effectiveness of training, to ensure that the best use is being made of resources or for planning purposes. The most cost-effective training will be that which provides the most benefits or has the greatest impact on lives of people, for the least cost. The cost-effectiveness of training depends to a large extent on the approach taken by the implementing agency. In the Bangladesh case study, the most cost-effective approach has been to train fieldworkers from development organizations, who then pass on the knowledge to the food

Talking to the beneficiaries is invaluable in determining the success and relevance of the training course (IT/Keith Machell)

processors and ultimate project beneficiaries. In the Uganda case study, it was cost-effective to train individuals who are already involved in a small-scale enterprise.

> *Cost-effective analysis and cost-benefit analysis.*
> **Cost-effectiveness** assesses the costs of achieving the outputs of a project. For example, the cost per training course, cost per person trained, cost per job created. It does not place a value on these outputs.
> **Cost-benefit** analysis attempts to place a value on the outputs and compare that to the costs of training. It is, therefore, more complex and more subjective than an analysis of the cost-effectiveness.

Assessment of cost-effectiveness

The first step is to assess both direct and indirect costs related to the training. For example, staff salaries, rent and rates and overhead costs, plus fees for course trainers, training workshop and course materials. At the most basic level, the cost per trainee can easily be calculated by dividing the total costs by the number of people trained. If, as is the case in the Bangladesh case study, the trainers pass on this information to the project beneficiaries, who in turn establish food processing businesses, a further analysis can be performed. The cost-effectiveness can be calculated as the total number of people with new skills or the number of businesses established. It will be more difficult to obtain accurate figures for these, but informed estimates of the numbers can be made by scaling up from a sample that is interviewed.

Time to allocate to evaluation

The time allocated to an evaluation will vary according to the amount of information to be collected. Rapid evaluations can be carried out at the end of each course. These will only take between one and two hours of discussion with the course participants. It is the time required afterwards that is more demanding, when the participants' opinions are noted and acted upon. The feedback may indicate that the training would benefit from modifications to the style or content of training sessions. A good trainer will take these comments on board and adapt the training to meet the participants' needs. This will obviously take time but it will be effort worth spending.

An impact assessment can be carried out after several training sessions to measure the effect of the training on the livelihoods of the individuals attending. It will require more time and inputs and these should not be underestimated. Sufficient time should also be allocated to the design of the questionnaire and other tools for collecting

The training programme initiated by IT Bangladesh resulted in the establishment of more than 1300 small businesses (IT/ Neil Cooper)

information. A good design ensures that relevant information is collected which will answer all the questions asked. The time needed to collect the information depends upon the size of the survey sample.

Sampling
There are many different ways of sampling, but for the purpose of this book two types are discussed as they should cover the majority of cases:

○ *Random samples* are chosen from the total pool of trained people. This can be done using a random numbers table or by placing the names of all potential samples in a bag and selecting the required number.
○ *Stratified samples* In some instances it may be desirable to deliberately choose groups of people to interview. In this case, the total pool of trained people is split into different categories – this may be according to age, location, type of business – and then a random sample is selected from within the different categories.

The following example illustrates the difference between the two types of sampling and when it may be more appropriate to use each type. In the Bangladesh case study (Chapter 5), a total of 103 people were trained at nine different courses. To obtain a purely random sample, the names of these 103 individuals should be placed in a bag and the first twenty (a 20 per cent sample) to be drawn out should be interviewed. Although this sample is random, it is possible that it will not represent all nine training courses. For example, the 20 names selected may all have attended courses one and two. To ensure that the views of participants from all nine courses are included – especially if the assessment aims to measure how the course developed and improved with time – the 103 participants must first be stratified into groups according to the course number. This will result in nine groups or strata, each containing on average 11 or 12 individuals. The final sample for surveying contains individuals, selected at random, from all nine groups. There are then two options for selecting the final sample:

○ select the final sample so that it represents the split of participants across groups; and
○ select the same number of individuals from each group.

Both methods are valid, it depends upon the objectives of the evaluation as to which method is chosen. Usually, if there is a big difference in the numbers in each stratum, a more representative picture would be obtained by selecting a sample based on the weighting. However, when there is little difference in stratum size, it is sufficient to take a sample of equal size from each group.

For example, in Figure 4.2, there is an uneven split of participants across the nine courses. When a sample is selected from the stratified groups, it could be chosen to

Course number	1	2	3	4	5	6	7	8	9
Number of participants	5	10	20	15	7	9	12	8	17

Figure 4.2 *Stratification of course participants according to training course number*

represent the split, for example select three times as many participants from the fourth course as the first course and so on. Alternatively, the same number can be selected from all nine groups regardless of the unequal split.

Sample size

The size of the sample taken varies according to the size and variability within the total group. The larger the variability, the larger the sample will need to be in order to get a realistic cross-section. Variability means the number of different groups represented within the total sample. For a large total group of, say, 100 000 individuals, it will be adequate to interview a 1 per cent or 5 per cent sample. However, for a smaller group of, say, 100 individuals, it is necessary to interview a larger sample of 15 to 20 per cent to get accurate information. It may be useful to take advice from a statistician.

Report writing

Evaluation and impact assessment are only worthwhile exercises if the recommendations are acted upon. It is essential to analyse and collate the data and to present it in a form which is interesting, clear and easy to understand. Diagrammatic representations, for example pie charts, bar charts and line graphs are more informative than numbers presented in tables, as the reader can immediately see the trends in the data.

It is inevitable that an evaluation will yield copious amounts of information. The author needs to distil out the most significant findings and present these in a concise summary, as it is likely that the summary will be the only part of the document that is read in any detail. The author should also make the report accessible to a range of readers. This may entail writing the summary report several times to allow for different levels of literacy and technical capacity. While writing the report, the author should not assume that the reader has any previous knowledge of the training course and should take care not to overlook details which are considered to be basic.

The findings of the evaluation should be fed back to those who supplied the information – the participants. They will feel that their time was put to good use and will feel that their contributions were worthwhile. They will also be interested in hearing the outcome of the evaluation and the recommendations which arise from it. The best way to feedback the information is by holding workshops where the participants can play an active part.

It is a pointless exercise to write a report and file it away to gather dust. Whatever the findings of the evaluation, they should be disseminated to a wide audience unless the funders have stressed that the information is confidential. The evaluation or impact assessment should highlight important lessons which others can learn from. If there were aspects of the training that were unsuccessful or inappropriate, other trainers should be aware of them. Likewise, successful approaches should be made available to others so they can be replicated.

Follow-up

Follow-up should be an essential element of all training programmes. Without a coherent follow-up policy, training will be less effective than it could be. It has often been said that '80 per cent of the success of a training programme is the follow-up', and this has been highlighted in many of the case studies in this book.

Visiting the trainees in the field is the best way to sort out potential problems (IT/Neil Cooper)

Follow-up has a dual purpose. It is an essential means of assisting trainers from training of trainers courses or entrepreneurs after completion of training. It is also one of the most effective ways of monitoring the usefulness of the course in order to adapt and design courses. As the case study from Peru states:

'The implementation of the follow-up system as a part of after-course evaluation has been of great help to the course organizers. It has allowed a better screening of participants and also provides timely technical assistance in collaboration with institutions sharing common goals.'

It is often a daunting task for extension workers or entrepreneurs to put into practice what they have learned at a training course. Follow-up can greatly increase the confidence of trainers and can help to sort out problems as they arise.

Components of follow-up

It is essential that follow-up support does not just concentrate on narrow technical aspects but also on the skills and knowledge needed to identify and develop the right product, the ability to respond to changes in the market and to promote and market the product. This support may be supplied by the trainer, as cited in the Sri Lanka and Peru case studies (Chapters 11 and 9), or alternatively by local consultants, as described in the Uganda case study (Chapter 13). A follow-up programme should include the following components.

The type of support required will vary between individuals, but the following were the most commonly asked for in follow-up sessions from the case studies:

○ business design;
○ business management;
○ business evaluation;
○ specific food technologies;
○ technical modification;
○ storage techniques;
○ supply and commissioning of equipment;
○ packaging and labelling;
○ marketing of the product; and
○ transfer of the knowledge to others.

In addition to direct support to entrepreneurs, trainers can also provide indirect support by influencing policymakers, governmental officials, credit officers, standards organizations and business associations to provide a more favourable environment for the intended beneficiaries.

Fieldworkers are more likely to request further support in training techniques and methods of passing on knowledge they have acquired, whereas entrepreneurs will usually be more concerned about technical and managerial problems specific to their own business. Each situation demands a unique type of support. For example, the requirements of fieldworkers differ from those of an entrepreneur. Similarly, there is a difference in the form of support required by literate and illiterate individuals. Different ways of offering support include:

○ refresher courses;
○ written technical reply service;
○ visits to an information centre;
○ workshops;
○ networks;
○ field visits at intervals; and
○ one-to-one support.

Follow-up for fieldworkers

It is essential for a training programme to provide on-going support to trainers or fieldworkers after a course in order to build on the skills they have acquired. This can be done by:

○ the training organization providing support in the field;
○ the fieldworkers' organization providing support in the field;
○ follow-up workshops;
○ mutually supportive networks; and
○ specific centres of support and information.

The majority of case studies in this book have specific programmes of follow-up in the field planned as part of the training programmes. The visits should be informal and the trainer should allow the fieldworker to set the pace and agenda. It is important to document the visit to keep a record of points raised and use these to improve the course.

In the case study from Bangladesh, the trainers aim to visit at least 50 per cent of all fieldworkers at their work sites within six months of completing the course and again after two years. In a recent evaluation, participants requested more follow-up support from the training organization, especially in specified technical areas. This request has been addressed by organizing two- to three-day courses concentrating on specific food products. As the visits are usually a few months after the course, the fieldworkers have had time to put their learning into action. Field visits also provide the trainers with a better understanding of the real problems faced by the entrepreneurs.

Fieldworkers need technical and financial support and commitment from their organization to put the skills they have acquired into practice. Sometimes this does not happen and fieldworkers are sent on training courses as a form of reward, or in other cases the organization may not understand the full implications of the support required after training has finished. The training organization has a number of ways of addressing this problem:

o no free training and screening of participants;
o building-up a relationship with the sending organizations; and
o modular courses so that participants can leave if the training does not meet their expectations before embarking on the second module.

It is important that some charge is made for attending courses to dissuade less serious participants and organizations. The training courses in both the Bangladesh and Sri Lanka case studies charge a fee which covers room, board and materials. In the Peru case study, charges aim to cover trainers' salaries and material costs, and in Uganda the eventual aim is full cost recovery. Good working relationships should be developed with all sending organizations. In the case study from Bangladesh, workshops have been held with policymakers from development organizations to discuss the need to support small-scale food processing enterprises.

Another interesting approach is to split courses into phases, as in the Sri Lankan case study. The financial implications of training for the organization are quantified in monetary terms and presented to participants at the outset. In addition, other implications such as time and resource requirements for the sending organization are discussed. Participants and their organizations can then consider whether they want to continue with training.

Post-course workshops also provide an opportunity for fieldworkers to meet, share experiences, raise common concerns and work through specific problems. The case studies from South Africa, Sri Lanka and Bangladesh mention the use of regional workshops.

An effective way of supporting fieldworkers is to create networks to provide mutual support, as has been done in the Sri Lankan case study. The trainers act as resource persons to each other and through regular meetings, share experiences and ideas which motivate them to be innovative and active. This allows IT Sri Lanka to

A range of products from the Sudanese Women Development Society (IT/Mohammed Majzoub)

diversify training and reduce the dependency on one set of trainers. It also helps the trainees to gain professional experience and extend this to their locality. In the Peru, Sri Lanka and Uganda case studies, centres have been established where fieldworkers can come and request support and information.

Follow-up for entrepreneurs

Visiting entrepreneurs in their workplace enables them to raise specific concerns face-to-face with the trainers. This allows the trainer to gain a fuller understanding of the context in which the entrepreneur operates. Short refresher courses or workshops for entrepreneurs are an effective way of supporting them. In the case study from South Africa, community workshops were held not just for participants but also for other interested people from the region.

Small-scale processors also benefit from joining a network or trade association of entrepreneurs involved in similar businesses. Together, they are more able to compete with the larger companies and can discuss specific technical problems, pool resources to purchase bulk supplies of raw materials or packaging material, and in some cases organize joint marketing. For example, the Women's Development Societies in the Sudan case study have established mutually supportive groups to carry out a variety of activities including improving marketing knowledge and skills; identifying new products; accessing raw materials; organizing credit and savings schemes and providing production information. Support centres can also offer invaluable technical and business management advice to small-scale entrepreneurs.

The issues covered in this and previous chapters are highlighted in the following case studies.

Case Studies

5
Food processing training in Bangladesh
SHAHEDA AZAMI, SUE AZAM-ALI and MIKE BATTCOCK

Introduction

Bangladesh is one of the world's poorest countries; however, its people are rich in ingenuity, skills and spirit. They live on the edge of a fragile economy, worsened by the unpredictable climatic conditions. More than 60 per cent of the 120 million population are 'functionally' landless; that is, they do not have access to sufficient land for subsistence. Each year, the population increases by around three million people, over two-thirds of whom are born into poverty. In the next 20 years the population is expected to double, further increasing the pressure on land and the number of landless. Consequently, what was once a predominantly agricultural economy is having to expand and provide alternative means of employment for the increasing labour force. Many people sell their labour in an increasingly competitive market and over 50 per cent of the workforce in rural areas are underemployed.

In the search for alternative, attractive forms of employment, food processing provides exciting, viable opportunities. Food processing is one of the most important sources of income and employment in Bangladesh, especially in rural areas where it is the main employer of women. Rice parboiling and hulling employs millions of women in the rural areas, where the annual turnover is an astounding US$500 million. The production of snack foods is another important sector in both rural and urban areas, providing employment opportunities for both men and women. In Manikganj, a town of 38 000 people, traditional street-food businesses have an annual turnover of US$2 million. Not only is the food processing sector crucial for the national economy, it is also one of the fastest growing sectors in Bangladesh, at 32 per cent per annum.

The need for training

It is obvious that food and food processing play an important role in Bengali culture. Walking through any bazaar it is impossible not to notice the many delights on offer – freshly cooked *paratha*, spicy *chatpotti*, tasty puffed rice, hot sticky *jelabi*, cool creamy *rass malai*. There is something to suit every taste and occasion. To find out where inputs would be of most value, Intermediate Technology (IT Bangladesh) carried out a survey of the food processing sector which reinforced the view that food processing was an important means of income generation for marginalized people. It also highlighted that not all small-scale businesses are successful because of a lack of business and technical knowledge and skills.

Snack foods are ideal for production on a small scale (IT/Mike Battcock)

These findings prompted IT Bangladesh, in collaboration with partner organizations, to develop a training course designed for fieldworkers assisting landless people to establish small-scale food processing businesses.

Objectives

The objective of the training courses is to assist landless people to improve their quality of life by increasing their income from sustainable small-scale food processing enterprises. This is achieved by transferring information and expertise in running food processing enterprises and influencing policymakers to improve the policy environment for such enterprises.

Developing the course

It was decided to design training courses for fieldworkers who would then work with the final beneficiaries. In this way the benefits of the course would extend to the largest number of people possible.

It was essential that the partner organizations were committed to food processing as an income-generating activity for their beneficiaries, that they had the human and financial resources to send their field staff for training and to allow the training to be put into practice. The partner organizations selected have a strong poverty focus and work with the functionally landless and asset-less (between 50 and 60 per cent of the population of Bangladesh); women and children, especially divorced and widowed women who are particularly vulnerable; and those on less than Tk200 (US$7) per month.

Selection of participants

IT Bangladesh works closely with the partner organizations to select suitable participants for the courses. In the past, the decision on who to send was largely left to the sending organization but this did not prove to be totally satisfactory. Often, friends and relatives were sent for training as a favour. These individuals had no intention of returning to the field to carry out training and were only at the course as a status symbol or reward. To ensure that only those who are committed to training attend the courses, IT Bangladesh charges a fee to cover board and lodging and now plays a more active role in screening potential candidates.

Location of the course

At the outset it was decided that the course would be held at different locations throughout Bangladesh. This makes it more accessible to people from remote locations who may find it difficult or impossible to travel far from home. For women it is often difficult to leave home for long periods because of their childcare and household duties and because of religious constraints. Also, it is more useful for the trainers if they see the environment in which the trainees will be operating, for example the proximity to markets and the availability of raw materials. In this way they can gain a fuller understanding of the likely constraints and they can tailor the training to suit the particular situations.

Training facilities

Training is usually carried out in an office or other suitable building. There is no purpose-built training centre, as the course organizers intended the situation to be as close to that which the fieldworkers and beneficiaries will encounter in the field. In Bangladesh, most of the small-scale processors work from their homes. To present them with sophisticated buildings and electrical equipment would be totally inappropriate and have the effect of disheartening them. The aim is to convince women that they have the capability to produce high-quality products using the resources they have available and to teach them appropriate skills which will enable this. The majority do not have access to sophisticated equipment and rely on equipment which is available in their homes or the local market. The courses now make a deliberate effort to avoid using balances and instead introduce more appropriate ways of measuring out quantities.

Shingara

1. Prepare ingredients

1.25kg flour
1kg potato
1kg coconut
500g onion
250g garlic
250g peanuts
2 to 3 pieces of green chilli
Small amount of coriander leaf
1/2 teaspoon of turmeric
1/2 teaspoon of coriander powder
Oil (soybean)

2. Mixing

Mix a little salt and 50g oil with the flour and add water to make dough. Peel potatoes and cut into small pieces. Split a fresh coconut, cut into small pieces (1cm). Mix in turmeric powder, coriander, garlic, onion and coconut pieces with the potato. Fry this mixture in oil. Mix peanuts with cooked potato mixture (vegetables such as beans, cauliflowers, carrots may also be added to flavour). Cool cooked potato mixture.

3. Shaping

Take a small ball (2cm in diameter) of dough and roll it. Cut into two pieces and fold each piece in half along the straight edge, pinching the edges together to close. Keeping the round edge upward pour some potato mixture into the hole. Close the round edge over the other corners to make it look like a triangle. Heat the oil in a deep pan and fry *shingara* until crisp and brown in colour. Allow to cool and serve with sauce.

4. Packaging

Generally none is needed. People sell fresh *shingara* in the market.

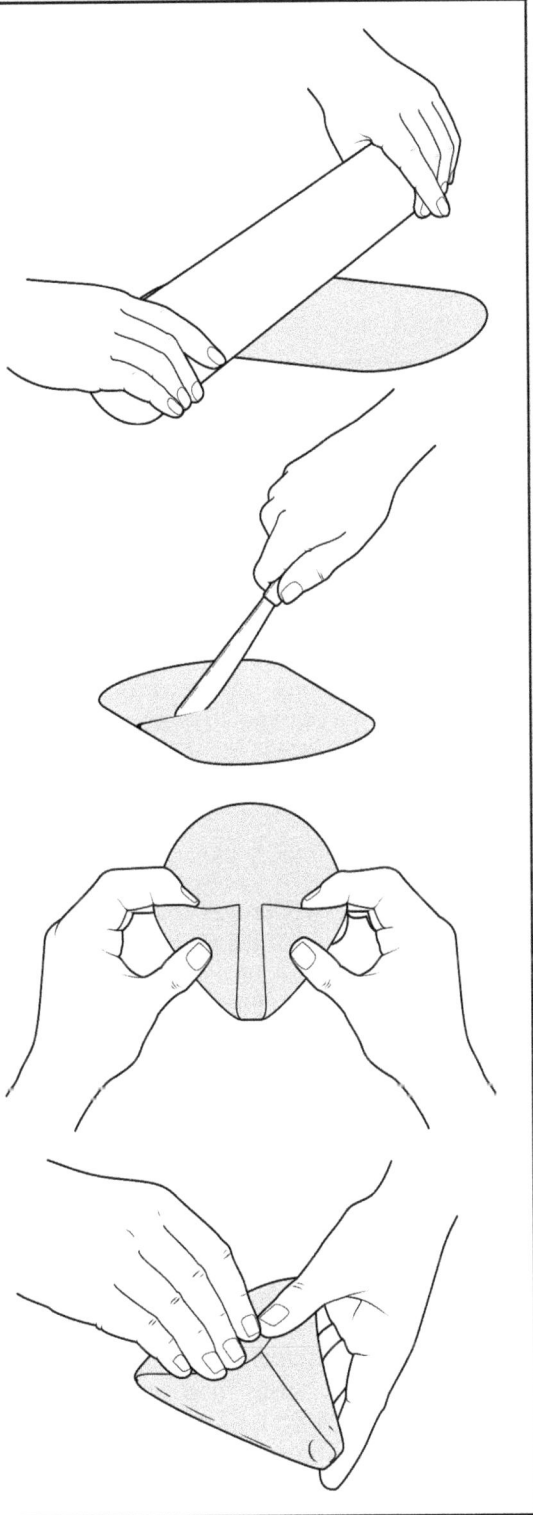

Figure 5.1 *The production of a typical Bangladeshi snack,* shingara

Food technology	Business
Food and nutrition	Sales, cost, profit
Food processing techniques	Stocks, accounts
Causes of food spoilage	Depreciation costs: variable, fixed
Food preservation	Balance sheet: liabilities, assets
Hygiene	Break even analysis
Quality control	Cash flow forecasting
Raw material preparation	Costing and pricing
Packaging	Bookkeeping
	Market survey
	Management report writing
	Business plan writing and finalization

Table 5.1 *Course content for food processing training in Bangladesh*

Some of the training sessions are held in small-scale commercial facilities to give the trainers an insight into production on a slightly larger scale. The ones used in the past have been *shingara* producers and bakeries. Professional food processors (including sweet makers, *channa chur* and *shingara* makers) have also been invited onto the course to enable participants to learn about practical problems faced in the market place.

Course content

The training courses cover the topics outlined in Table 5.1. Most of the ultimate beneficiaries of the training course are illiterate women. Therefore the fieldworkers are taught numerous techniques for transferring the technical and business information as part of the sessions below. This includes the use of songs, games and illustrated flipcharts, especially for the sessions on hygiene and food safety.

The sessions on food technology cover a range of food products including jam, jelly, *mishti* (sweetmeats), *shingara* (vegetable mixture in pastry snack food product), cakes, biscuits, bread, *channa chur* (mixed nut and fried dough snack food product) and pickles (*see* Figure 5.1).

For the small-scale processor, it may seem irrelevant to include sessions on business management, cash flow and accounting. However, as all successful entrepreneurs are aware, financial management and planning are essential tools for the smooth running of any business. Of course, the business sessions should be tailored to the needs of the particular audience (of which the majority in Bangladesh are semi-literate or illiterate). At this scale of production, simple bookkeeping and cash flow statements are sufficient. To overcome difficulties and to present the business sessions in a friendly, easy to understand form, the team in Bangladesh adopted the CARE 'five finger' approach to finance and accounts into the course. The five finger approach is a participatory and entertaining method of conveying the five basic elements of a successful business to illiterate groups of people. It avoids technical language and relies heavily on repetition and memory through role play and participation. Each finger represents one of the important aspects of business planning and management which are essential for a successful business to run profitably (*see* Figure 5.2). Fieldworkers often found the business sessions, particularly the sessions on cash flow and profit/loss accounting very difficult whilst the beneficiaries (the semi-literate/illiterate women processors) excelled. This latter group often did the business accounts and arithmetic in their heads but had more problems transferring them to paper.

Short courses

In the last two years, there has been a move towards short three- to five-day courses which address specific issues. These short

> **The five finger approach**
>
> The following five questions are asked whilst holding and then crossing each of the fingers:
>
> 1. Do I know the technology or skill needed for the product I intend to make?
> 2. Where will I sell the products I intend to produce?
> 3. Will I make a profit?
> 4. Do I have the money to start the venture. If not, can I get credit or a loan?
> 5. Will I be able to contribute some money to my family?

Figure 5.2 *The elements of the 'five finger' approach*

courses are designed as refresher courses or back-up support for the fieldworkers already trained. They are organized by IT Bangladesh at the request of partner organizations. To date, four short courses have been held covering cheese, *channa chur*, toffee and tomato sauce and pickles. It is likely that this approach will be the way forward for training in Bangladesh, as it is proving more effective to support and upgrade the skills of those who have proved themselves in the field of agro-processing than to continue training newcomers.

Monitoring

At the start of each course, participants express their expectations which allows the technical components of the course to be modified according to their needs. A pre-training exercise is carried out to establish the knowledge level of participants. This is repeated at the end of the course to measure the effectiveness of transferring information. During the course, participants are asked to report back daily on what they have learnt. Two trainees are selected each day and asked to make a short presentation to the group on what they consider to be the key learning point from that day. This type of feedback enables the trainers to gauge the pace and level of the course and to improve subsequent modules. It is an invaluable tool in monitoring the effectiveness of the training methods employed. Through this regular monitoring of the course and taking into account the opinions and requests from fieldworkers, beneficiaries and

Participants learn about business management and planning using the 'five-finger' approach (IT/Alamgeer Haque)

partner organizations, there has been a steady improvement in the course over the years. There is still scope for further improvement, as indicated by the requests from the fieldworkers.

Impact of the training

Throughout Bangladesh nine training courses have been held, training 103 fieldworkers from 46 development organizations. Two participative workshops, where trained fieldworkers meet and share their experiences, have been held in Dhaka. In 1993, an evaluation was carried out which recommended that more time was allocated to follow-up and the support of fieldworkers. A second evaluation was carried out in 1996 to determine the impact of the course on the

> **The impact of training on Minoti Ghosh**
>
> Minoti Ghosh lives in a slum area of Dhaka called Lakhi Bazar. She is married with one daughter and three sons. Before she set up her business, the family lived in a single room measuring 10 feet square. Her husband worked in a mishti (sweetmeat) workshop, earning only Tk40 per day which is insufficient to keep a family of five in Dhaka. She could not afford to send her children to school.
>
> Minoti became a member of the Church of Bangladesh women's group where she received training and advice on how to set up a small business from fieldworkers who had trained on one of the IT Bangladesh training courses. After support in developing a business plan, she received a Tk2000 loan which she repaid weekly over two months at 2 per cent interest.
>
> Minoti decided to set up a small business making a range of food products, including *shingara* (like a samosa), *peajo* (a dried lentil biscuit), cutlet (potato and meat snack) and ready to eat breakfast meals of paratha and vegetables. The business proved to be so successful that her husband left his job to help her. She rented a small shop-front nearby for Tk1200 a month from where she could sell the products. As the business became more established her daughter also joined her. Her husband now travels once a week to a rural market in Adalpur (about one hour from Dhaka) to buy the raw materials they use. These cost Tk1000 for each day's production.
>
> Minoti starts preparing the foods at 9 a.m. and does not finish until 11p.m. She and her daughter produce 80 pieces of at least four of the different products. She has a single gas ring to cook on which costs her Tk250 a month. To start with she used her own domestic utensils but now, with the profits from the business she has bought a wide range of pots, pans and equipment. She is very careful about hygiene to ensure that her products are of high quality. Her husband sells these products for at least Tk2000 every day.
>
> The training course and the success of the business have had an incredible impact on Minoti and her family. They have been able to buy a second room to live in and are the proud owners of two radios and a fan. Two of her sons can now attend school, which greatly improves their chances in life. They are satisfied with the business and have no ambition to expand further as they want to keep the business in the family.

intended beneficiaries and to measure the progress towards meeting the objectives.

Direct benefits
- 87 per cent of the fieldworkers trained are actively involved in food processing;
- they have passed on their skills and advice to over 5000 beneficiaries;
- 1300 of the beneficiaries have established successful small-scale enterprises;
- these provide employment to 6500 people;
- the 6500 beneficiaries benefit by US$1.3 million each year.[1]

The training project has had a tremendous impact on the livelihoods of the beneficiaries. As a result of the extra income raised from agro-processing businesses, families have seen significant improvements in their lives. For instance, some families now send their children to school and others have opted to improve their homes, bought land or live-

[1] The average weekly profit of businesses is Tk872. Calculated at a working year of three hundred days, this amounts to a daily profit of Tk151 (US$5-6 per day). Compared to the manual labourer who earns around Tk30 (about a dollar) for a strenuous day's labour breaking bricks or carrying out agricultural work, this is a very desirable wage. Over one year, an average business earns about Tk45 344. Multiplied by the number of successful businesses (1300), this gives a total figure of Tk58 947 200 profit, which is equivalent to US$1.9 million.

Channa chur *is one of the most popular products made by small-scale processors; trainees learn how to make it to a higher quality (IT/Neil Cooper)*

stock with the extra income. All these contribute to increased security for the family.

Small-scale agro-processing is particularly suited to women since it can be carried out in the home concurrent with the other household activities. The project evaluation highlighted the significant number of women who have benefited from the training and the subsequent increases in income and security. Although the project focuses on supporting women as they are traditionally the most disadvantaged group in this society, men are not excluded from the training. Male members of the family continue to play a role in the small businesses through assistance with the purchase of raw materials and marketing the products. They also benefit from the increased family income and the improvement in livelihoods, as is illustrated by the case of Minoti Ghosh (see box).

Along with the increased income comes increased confidence and respect from family members and within the community. This increased respect and empowerment of women makes it easier for women to raise awareness amongst fellow women.

Cost-effectiveness

The cost per successful enterprise has been calculated at an average US$66 and cost per final beneficiary at US$7 which is considered to be very cost-effective. The course has improved its effectiveness at meeting the beneficiaries' needs by tenfold reduction in costs (from US$560 to US$66) per enterprise established over the last three years.

Indirect benefits

Most of the products are produced and marketed locally, using raw materials and equipment available in the local market. This localized production has a positive impact on the rural economy through supporting local suppliers of raw materials and the creation of profitable, alternative employment in the rural areas. The creation of sustainable small businesses in rural areas can help to stem the flow of urban migration. By producing and marketing goods locally, there is no need for transport which keeps the production costs low. In addition, because the food products are prepared at home, using kitchen equipment, the overheads are low. These benefits are passed on to consumers as low-price, high quality food products.

Lessons learnt

Participant selection

It is essential to work with partner organizations who are committed to working on agro-processing with their beneficiaries and who have sufficient resources to support both their field staff and the beneficiaries. Careful selection of the fieldworkers to be trained is essential to ensure that they have the ability and are committed to passing on their skills to the beneficiaries.

Find out what people are doing and help them to do it better

The concentration on small-scale processing and traditional products with local markets have been important in the success of the training. All training should be based on the needs of the participants and should be relevant to the individual situation. New technologies should be developed in collaboration with beneficiaries and partners, building on their knowledge and skills.

Marketing

Marketing is one of the most serious constraints faced by small-scale processors. Competition with bigger manufacturers and against established brands makes it difficult for the small-scale processor to enter the market. However, there is a niche market which the small-scale processor can and does target to good effect. It is not feasible for IT Bangladesh as a charity to consider marketing the products, despite numerous requests from beneficiaries and partner organizations. Our approach is to act as a facilitator, establishing contacts and market links and providing information to both the processor and the customer.

Working with entrepreneurs

Now that over 100 fieldworkers have been trained and passed on their skills to over 5000 people, it has been found to be more beneficial to support and upgrade the skills of those already trained, than to extend training to newcomers. Similarly with the beneficiaries, those who show some entrepreneurial spirit and initiative are more likely to succeed than total newcomers.

Collaborating with the formal sector

There is tremendous potential for collaboration, but a large communication gap exists between the large- and small-scale processors. IT Bangladesh can fill this gap with the production of suitable information.

Access to credit

Access to credit is essential to enable trainees to establish small-scale enterprises. IT Bangladesh must work with partner organizations who can provide credit and regular back-up support to the beneficiaries.

Gender sensitivity

The dual productive and reproductive roles of women are taken into account during the planning and implementation of the training courses. The training is carried out by a female member of staff who is sympathetic to the needs of women and the numerous demands on their time.

Further reading

The following reports are available from IT Bangladesh or the IT head office in the UK:

1. 'Agro-processing sector survey', Ahmed, C.S. (1989), IT Bangladesh.
2. 'Evaluation and impact assessment of the Intermediate Technology training course in Bangladesh', Azami, S. and Battcock, M. (1993), IT Bangladesh.
3. 'Training for livelihood security', Azami, S., Brough, S. and Battcock, M. (1996), IT Bangladesh.

6
PRODAR's experience in management training for rural agro-industry – the Central American example

FRANCOIS BOUCHER and MARVIN BLANCO

Introduction

Rural agro-industry is understood to be any action which adds value to agricultural production through post-harvest activities such as storage, processing, transformation, conservation, packaging, transport or marketing. It is an interesting alternative method of improving the standard of living and income of small producers in Latin America and the Caribbean. According to studies carried out in the sector, there are at least five million enterprises in Latin America which can be considered part of the rural agro-industrial sector, between them producing more than 10 million tons of manufactured goods annually and providing around 20 million jobs. For the sake of improved efficiency and a better understanding of the topic, a distinction has been made between traditional, indigenous rural agro-industry and that which has come about through the efforts of development projects, which has been called induced rural agro-industry.

Traditional rural agro-industry has developed largely heterogeneously – a product of the agro-export model on which the majority of Latin American economies are based: the export of coffee, sugar, cocoa, meat and bananas, but marginalization of other sectors such as dairy produce or brown sugar, which have limited technological development and support.

Induced rural agro-industry refers to enterprises which have come about due to the encouragement and support of governmental and non-governmental organizations. This has had a positive impact on small producers, quantifiable in terms of income obtained, direct and indirect employment generated, and improved community development – better roads, electrification, financing. Amongst the most successful examples is the rural cheese factories project in Ecuador, which has benefited many Andean communities by integrating them into a production and marketing system of both fresh and matured cheeses. Another project worth mentioning is the cassava drying project which has brought about the creation of more than 400 rural agro-industries in Colombia, Ecuador and the north-east of Brazil. It is thought that such projects have created more than 750 induced rural agro-industries over the last 10 years and provided support services to around 100 000 traditional rural agro-industries, mainly in the sugar sector (brown sugar/molasses), cheese factories, grains and other Andean products such as honey bottling and processing of fruits, colorants and spices.

PRODAR and training

The Co-operative Programme of Rural Agro-industrial Development (PRODAR) was set up in 1989 as a programme of research and development. The aim of PRODAR is to strengthen, encourage and establish rural agro-industries in Latin America and the Caribbean through networking and integration of the efforts of national and international organizations. PRODAR's activities are concentrated around four principal axes: the creation and strengthening of National Networks for Rural Agro-Industry (REDAR – networks have been set up in 15 Latin American and Caribbean countries), research, training and information-documentation.

Training, an essential element in the development of rural agro-industry

In 1984, when the first international seminar on rural agro-industry took place in Costa Rica (organized by RETADAR, the Network for Appropriate Technology for the Development of Rural Agro-Industry), training at all levels was identified as one of the greatest constraints for rural agro-industry: training of trainers, training of peasants and training of rural, small-business people. This situation was confirmed when studies on rural agro-industry were carried out in several countries in the region. These studies highlighted serious deficiencies amongst those people running enterprises, such as:

o the design of commercial projects;
o the establishment of accounting systems and financial analysis;
o the development of new projects, health and sanitation systems and quality control; and
o the implementation of appropriate technology in a rural environment.

These studies also showed that those working in rural agro-industrial enterprises had few opportunities to obtain training in these disciplines since no one offered programmes targeted at rural agro-industry and, because of their rural location, many business people found it difficult to attend training courses that were held far from their place of work. In addition, for the majority of institutions involved in the development of rural agro-industry, training in the agro-industrial sector was a new venture. Consequently, they had little experience and few trained staff who were able to undertake a mass training programme.

For these reasons, both the RETADAR network, and PRODAR focused largely on training and the provision of appropriate courses. ERTEC courses (Reflection Spaces for Technologists) began in 1986 which were aimed at the training of technical staff involved in the promotion and support of rural agro-industry. Although 10 such courses were organized between 1987 and 1990 in various Latin American countries (four in the Andean region: Bolivia, Colombia, Ecuador and Peru), their success was limited by a lack of adequate resource materials and the lack of subsequent follow up of participants.

A new approach to training

In 1991, PRODAR embarked on a scheme to improve the courses so that they more fully met the needs of the participants. Liberalization and the opening up of new markets in Latin America offered many opportunities, but the small-scale rural agro-processors found it difficult to compete due to their limited capacity for development and lack of information.

The new approach included a training project which was aimed at improving the capacity of rural agro-industrial managers and leaders in the areas of project planning, administration, accounting, marketing, processing technology and product quality. It would be designed to equip all participants with the minimum knowledge necessary to manage their agro-industrial enterprise effectively.

To try and ensure sustainability of the training, a second stage of the project was also proposed. This was designed to support institutions in developing the courses and to establish a capacity for extension training which would provide follow-up support and advice to the trained people and which could follow-up new requests.

PRODAR's project, as developed in Central America

As a result, in 1991 PRODAR established a project 'Management training for rural agro-industry'. The overall objective of this project was to establish a programme of ongoing and systematic training which would generate business awareness and expertise and enable sustained development of the rural agro-industrial sector in Central America and the Caribbean (Dominican Republic).

The following specific objectives were established:

o to provide the national institutions in charge of training with a package of teaching materials covering the different topics of concern to rural agro-industries;
o to train a group of trainers and professionals in the organization, promotion and development of training activities for rural agro-industries;
o to support the organization of courses in each country which would serve to validate the training package;
o to design a strategy for institutional co-operation which would provide, on a national level, support for the launch of, and follow-up to, the activities to be initiated through the project.

A new methodology

A new and innovative methodology was implemented to carry out this training project:

o in the manner that the technical elements of the course were presented;
o in that the trainers were trained not only in technical issues but also in the management of training (how to train and how to organize courses);
o in its participative and integrated approach – during the courses, participants have the chance to design their own projects, create an enterprise or suggest improvements to their existing venture;
o in the innovative design of its follow-up mechanisms.

Above all, the integrated character of the training package, including managerial and commercial vision, must be highlighted. In the same way that there has been a rapid evolution in the conceptual framework of rural agro-industry, there has been a similar evolution in the training framework. Fifteen years ago, when the focus of rural agro-industry was merely technological, the corresponding courses were, above all, technological. It was thought in those days that one could help small producers by teaching them how to make jam and that this was sufficient! Later it was realized that what was important was to help them set up and run enterprises and thus the idea of the management package was born. As time passed, themes such as the role of women in rural agro-industry, sustainability and producers' organizations were incorporated. Today, due to the international climate of globalization and the opening up of markets, the package is being completed with a strong section on marketing as well as quality control in a competitive setting.

The first phase of the project

The first phase of the training project, known as 'Promotion of rural agro-industry in Central America and the Dominican Republic' commenced in May 1992. This group of countries was selected because of their similar geographical and socio-economic characteristics. This phase entailed the training of a first contingent of 60 trainers in how to use the package. The direct beneficiaries of the training were 25 institutions who work on training and technical assistance for rural agro-industrial enterprises. The indirect beneficiaries were the managers, leaders and heads of production and quality control of the co-operatives, producers' associations and family or individual enterprises.

The project was structured around three modules, through which it endeavoured to cover the issues involved in the day-to-day running of a rural agro-industrial enterprise. The modules are:

o The promotion of rural agro-industrial ventures.
o Administrative, financial and commercial management of rural agro-industries.

> **The preparation of training manuals, and their use**
>
> The methodology that was followed for the preparation and validation of the teaching materials can be summed up as follows:
>
> 1. Defining the training needs on the basis of problems identified through numerous research programmes and suggestions from specialists in the subject.
> 2. Defining the contents of the training package around three teaching modules: promotion of rural agro-industrial ventures; administrative, financial and commercial management of rural agro-industries and technological management and quality control in rural agro-industry.
> 3. Drawing up the technical manuals: specialists were contracted to write the technical materials.
> 4. Educational needs: specialists were contracted to put the technical contents in an appropriate educational format.
> 5. Training of trainers workshops: one workshop was carried out for each module. Each workshop had the objective of validating the manuals; training was as much on technical themes as on how to use the package and how to manage training courses. One workshop took place each year for three years.
> 6. Technical and educational changes suggested by the participants were incorporated.
> 7. Training of trainers workshops: following these changes, two workshops in the use of modules I and II were carried out which acted as a second validation.
> 8. Further corrections were incorporated.
> 9. Publication of the manuals which could be adapted by institutions to the conditions and requirements of each country. A user's guide and a rural agro-industry promotional video were also published.
> 10. In-country courses were organized in the countries, using this first package.
> 11. Follow-up and feedback: a follow-up process was initiated in each country in order to institutionalize the courses and to move towards a second stage of the project. A bulletin called 'Creating Agro-Industry' was published and a regional training network was set up.

o   Technological management and quality control in rural agro-industrial ventures.

The first and second modules have been printed and distributed. Three of the four manuals of the third module have just been published.

The National University of Costa Rica granted a university certificate to professionals having participated in the three modules of the course. During the stages of writing, educational input and publication of the manuals, technical and financial support were provided by the Training Division of IICA and of 'French Technical Co-operation', whilst for the organization of trainers' courses, support was provided by the 'Regional Belgian Co-operation'.

Main achievements

Amongst the main achievements of the project, the following should be highlighted:

o   the creation of a participative methodology for the development of training activities within the rural agro-industrial sector. The institutions were involved from the outset, participating in the design of the course content, materials for the manuals and field testing;

- the publication of 11 training manuals, one promotional video, exercises, case studies and a user's guide;
- organizing two courses in Costa Rica to validate the first and second modules and the training of 38 trainers in the region;
- organizing one course in Guatemala to validate the third module, and the training of 32 trainers in the region;
- organizing two courses in Guatemala, where 60 trainers were trained in the use of modules one and two;
- institutions have carried out more than 12 training activities where the package has been used, in which more than 200 agro-industrial business people have been trained;
- organizing a network of 25 institutions which provide training activities;
- increased awareness of new institutions in rural agro-industry as a means of developing rural areas;
- publication of the bulletin *Creating Agro-industry*, which disseminates information regarding the project activities;
- creation of CICAR in Costa Rica – the Inter-Institutional Commission for Rural Agro-industrial Training – which recently gained funding from the Dutch Government to commence a training project in Costa Rica. In the space of 18 months, 18 courses were carried out along with follow-up and support.

Conclusions

PRODAR has been able to develop a package of management training manuals for small rural businesses which have a new methodology. This package is being revised taking into account the experience acquired during the development of the project in Central America and the Dominican Republic, but also taking into account the current climate of globalization of agro-industry, opening up of markets and competitiveness. Nowadays, the way in which products are presented, how they are packed, and the labelling, are all as important (or even more so) than the product itself!

Now, PRODAR is able to produce and disseminate teaching materials on all issues of concern to small rural enterprises, organize training of trainers workshops and complementary courses in teaching techniques and design training activities. We can also advise on the implementation of our teaching materials. This project is available for use in the Andean region and PRODAR is ready to provide technical support for its transfer and adaptation to the region, be it a coastal, forest or mountain environment.

Figure 6.1   *Example of a PRODAR training manual*

7
Training in food processing – a sustainable approach in India
J.D. JOHN JAYARAJ

Introduction

Teaching the art of catching a fish requires more effort than merely giving a fish to a hungry man. However, once the techniques have been learnt, they remain with the individual for a lifetime. He is able to continue catching fish, whereas the hungry man had his hunger satisfied for one day only. There is a general, widespread opinion that non-governmental organizations are meant for charity; however the financial and funding agencies do not share this view – they always ask about the viability and sustainability of any project. These criteria can only be fulfilled when adequate and appropriate training is provided to the potential entrepreneurs. Training helps them to acquire more knowledge and skills and to yield better results.

The Palmyrah Workers' Development Society (PWDS)

The Palmyrah Workers' Development Society is a registered Voluntary Organization established in 1977. The society was initiated with the broad objective of improving the socio-economic conditions of downtrodden palmyrah workers, women and children in Kanyakumari and Trivandrum Districts of Tamil Nadu and Kerala States respectively. Empowerment through community organization and awareness raising was achieved by various participative development programmes with the community. These programmes included community health, skills training, resource mobilization, shelter development, product development, product promotion and entrepreneurship

Jaggery is a suitable product for small-scale production (IT/Mike Battcock)

development. They all have a particular emphasis on self-reliance.

Palmyrah

Palmyrah is a palm tree which grows in several countries including India, China, Sri Lanka, Bangladesh, Indonesia, Malaysia, Thailand and Nepal. In India, the trees are more abundant in the Southern States of Tamil Nadu, Andhra Pradesh, Kerala and

Karnataka. The palmyrah tree gives a sweet sap called *neera* from its flowers. The palmyrah workers collect the sweet sap and make it into a solid sweetener called *jaggery*. There are 500 thousand families engaged in palmyrah work in Tamil Nadu alone.

Palmyrah workers

In general, palmyrah workers and their families are poor and live in small thatched huts. Their main occupation of palmyrah tapping and processing is neither remunerative nor safe. It is a seasonal and accident-prone occupation which usually involves the whole family. The tapper climbs to the top of the tree to collect the *neera*, usually twice a day. The woman carries the *neera* from the bottom of the tree to the house and processes it. The children help the parents to transport the *neera*, collect the firewood and boil the *neera* to produce the *jaggery*. Sometimes the elder children are forced to look after the younger ones, which robs them of their childhood and denies them formal education.

Most of the palmyrah workers work for the landlords who own the tree and they are paid wages in kind (*neera*) on alternate days. On average a tapper can tap 30 to 40 trees and collect 50 to 80 litres of *neera* per day. The meagre income they earn from this occupation is inadequate to provide them with the most basic of family needs. In addition, they are not given proper recognition in society and are subject to discrimination by the other people.

The major reasons for their slow development are the following:

o The palmyrah workers are not organized.
o They only know how to produce the traditional (crude) form of *jaggery*, for which there is poor demand.
o They are exploited by middlemen in marketing their product. The price of *jaggery* is fixed by the traders and it is not fair to the primary producer.

Even though there is tremendous potential to increase employment opportunities, the palmyrah industry is in decline because of the poor remuneration now received by the artisans. This could be solved in two ways: producing alternative value-added products, such as palm candy, and devising new marketing strategies for palm products.

Palm product development

The studies and experience of PWDS reveal that it is impossible to improve the socio-economic conditions of the palmyrah artisans unless marketable value-added products are produced from *neera* instead of the traditional *jaggery*. In 1982, PWDS initiated research into alternative products through its palm product development programme. Laboratory experiments were conducted to try to eliminate the fermentation of *neera* and increase its shelf life so that it could be marketed as a nourishing natural soft drink. Some success was achieved but a uniform standard quality could not be obtained. More sophisticated microbiological research was necessary to obtain a quality product.

In the late 1980s, FAKT (Association for Appropriate Technology, Germany) began to work with PWDS to study more suitable alternative products such as refined *jaggery*, spiced *jaggery*, palm candy and palm syrup. After careful analysis of the situation, top priority was given to the production of palm candy, devising an appropriate technology and standardization of the process and product.

Palm Candy – an alternative value-added food product

Palm candy is a crystalline form of the sucrose in palm sap *neera*. It is a natural sweetener having both nutritive and medicinal values. The technology for producing palm candy is not complicated. After collecting the sweet sap from the tree top it is heated to 40°C then treated with lime and filtered. The pure *neera* is boiled to 108°C until it becomes a syrup of a specific viscosity. This boiled syrup is transferred to a specially designed container known as a 'crystallizer' and kept undisturbed for a period of at least 40 days for the natural process of crystallization to take place. Pearl-like palm candy crystals grow in the syrup. After extraction the crystals are cleaned and neatly packed. Since it is a natural, medicinal product, there is high demand for palm candy which can double the income of the artisans.

The transfer of technology

To transfer the technology from the lab to the field, a palmyrah worker group was identified in a particular village, Madichal. Initially, people were hesitant to adopt this new technology; however, after a series of discussions they agreed to try the process and the pilot project started in 1992. This was a learning experience for both the palmyrah workers and the technical team of PWDS. This attempt proved that the candy-making project is technically feasible and economically viable. After seeing the success of the Madichal candy unit, people from the nearby villages were keen to replicate the same model in their villages. At present five palm candy-making units are being managed successfully by the palmyrah artisans themselves.

In each unit, 10 to 15 palmyrah workers join together as producing partners. They regularly supply their *neera* to the centre and process it centrally. As soon as they supply *neera* to the centre, they are given Rs1.00 per litre as an advance to meet their daily needs. After selling the candy, each member is given a share of the profit in proportion to the *neera* supplied. Their income has doubled through candy making as compared to *jaggery* making.

Training approach

All training may not be suitable for all persons. When a particular training is designed and given to an individual who really requires it, the impact will be greater than if training is imposed on someone who does not require it. Our approach is to identify the needy and potential candidates and train them to become experts in the particular field and enhance their entrepreneurial skills. The training can be divided into three parts.

Pre-training. This is an essential pre-requisite to any training course. It involves the identification of trainees, the preparation of course content, sequence, design, duration and methodology, finalizing the venue and exploring the possibility of other support organizations.

Training. This is the actual delivery of training which includes both theoretical and practical aspects.

Post-training. This phase is centred on follow-up. The success of any training depends on how many persons have started their own production units. There may be some starting problems – for example setting up a production unit, gaining access to finance, fulfilling cumbersome government formalities and becoming established in the market place – where trainees need some counselling and encouragement. Many agencies do not give due weight to post training; however it should be regarded as inevitable and inseparable from the actual training.

In this case, the purpose of the training is to disseminate the palm candy-making technology to communities who are interested to start a community-based food candy-making unit. In the initial stage, PWDS staff visit the villages to attend the group meetings of the palmyrah workers and explain the benefits of palm candy-making. It usually takes around three to four months to convince the people to try making palm candy. Once they have decided to try the process, PWDS arranges training, provided they fulfil the following minimum requirements:

- there must be at least 10 to 15 palmyrah workers;
- they should regularly collect a minimum of 400 litres of *neera* per day; and
- they should give an undertaking that they will manage the unit, including appointment of candy-makers and providing infrastructural facilities.

The participatory training methodology used includes classroom study, group discussions, brainstorming, case study, demonstrations, experience sharing, exposure visits and on-the-spot placement.

Designing training courses

We have designed our training programme into three types, suitable for: trainers; members of a candy-making unit (producing partners); and technicians or candy-makers.

Trainers' training programme. This is solely designed for the NGO staff who are willing to replicate the community-based palm candy-making units in their target villages. The objectives are to provide orientation on initiating community-based palm candy-making and training for managing such operations.

The training content includes: orientation for a community-based income-generation programme, candy making and orientation for skills training, a comparative economic analysis of *jaggery* and palm-candy processing, technical feasibility and economic viability, the concept of a rural entrepreneurship development programme, entrepreneurial behaviour, how to prepare a business plan, appropriate technology, quality control, basic knowledge on initiating a production unit including environmental scanning, government formalities, marketing, record maintenance, management inputs, conducting base-line studies, monitoring and accompaniment, evaluation and follow-up. The methods used include classroom teaching, group discussions, experience sharing, exposure visits and on-the-spot training.

Training module for tappers. This course is an orientation to the members who are going to be involved in the candy making as producing partners. The duration of the training is two days. The trainees are given the basic concepts of entrepreneurship, project and product idea development, the advantages of palm-candy making, marketing, management and monitoring of the production unit. The training techniques include classroom input, experience sharing, group discussions and exposure visits.

Training for technicians and candy makers. The purpose of this training package is to impart the technology or skill. The course content includes the salient features of the raw material, the economic benefits of candy preparation, the process details, the precautions, the technology and installation of the unit. The duration of the training is 45 days, either continuous or in two modules because the end product, palm-candy, can only be harvested after 40 days of the natural crystallization process. After the successful completion of the training, the trainees become fully qualified technicians.

Evaluation and impact assessment

Evaluation is a tool to measure the effectiveness of the programme and enable the producing partners to improve further. We insist on participatory joint evaluation by the trainees and the evaluation team. Broadly speaking, the evaluation is carried out in two stages:

○ evaluation of trainees immediately after the training programme; and
○ performance evaluation of the unit after one year by the internal and external teams.

The tools used to monitor progress and impact are pre-training and post-training filled questionnaires and feedback by the trainees. On the other hand, in the performance evaluation the indicators are palmyrah workers' participation and co-operation, the quantity and quality of *neera* supplied, candy yield, quality control mechanisms, profitability, maintenance of accounts, dynamics in decision-making and degree of self-management.

The very purpose of the training is to enable the producing partners to manage their units by themselves. Managing a unit by a single person is comparatively easy, whereas managing a community-based unit by a group of members is very difficult. Here we apply the Participatory Impact Monitoring (PIM) mechanism. The impact assessment is a must for assisting a living industrial unit.

In the conventional method, an outsider is appointed to assess the impact of the unit. There are a lot of disadvantages in this process. The preconceived notions of the assessor may dilute the real growth and it also creates dependency on outside experts, who are more expensive. As a result, the producers are hesitant to conduct regular impact studies.

The participative impact monitoring is a simple monitoring tool to assess the impact effectively. Once the people are trained they can easily assess their strengths, weaknesses, success and failures every week by themselves using the indicators and make necessary corrections in their system to protect themselves from heavy loss or damage. In the candy-making units, the village people apply this method and it has proved successful. They prepare a monthly monitoring sheet and analyse the pros and cons and take remedial steps whenever necessary. The impact assessment has been carried out at two levels: unit-level impact monitoring and NGO-level impact monitoring. The impact of each unit is shared and reviewed in the joint reflection meeting of all the candy-making units promoted by PWDS. It gives more clarity and strength among the individual units. After seeing the successful application of PIM in candy units, many other NGOs have come forward to adopt this monitoring tool.

Conclusion

The systematic training and follow-up provided by PWDS in palm-candy making enables poor palmyrah workers to become efficient entrepreneurs. When the product quality has been improved by adding value through appropriate technology and training, people's power is also strengthened. Once a palmyrah worker only dreamt of having a hundred rupee note. Now they are handling hundreds of thousands of rupees through this food processing programme. In this situation, how can we deny that food processing training is not a strategy for sustainable development?

8
Food processing as a micro-business in Nepal
SABALA SHRESTHA

Introduction

This case study describes food processing businesses run by women in Nepal and the problems faced by female food processing entrepreneurs. Many people think that any woman can process food for business using their experience of home food preparation. However, entrepreneurs have to consider amongst other things the availability of raw materials, quality, packaging and consumers' interest and demand, before setting up their businesses.

Women constitute about half the population in Nepal, but much of their contribution remains unrecognized or taken for granted and they are often left out from any development activities. As a result, their status in society as well as their needs and concerns, both as agents and beneficiaries of development, have not been fully taken into consideration in development planning, nor in the formulation of policies and priority setting. The involvement of women accelerates development in a country like Nepal and it is stressed that development occurs only when both men and women participate equally.

The economy of Nepal is based on agriculture. As a result of growing difficulties in agriculture, efforts have to be made to divert the country's increasing population from agriculture to economically and technically viable industrial ventures. So enterprise development is needed for the economic development of the country and the economic empowerment of the people.

In rural, as well as urban areas, women make dried, fermented and fried products for their consumption. Adding some skill

Bakeries are among the most popular small businesses in Nepal (IT/R Velaochaga)

and knowledge of preservation, women can start a very small-scale micro food processing enterprise. In Nepal, according to a CBS (Central Bureau of Statistics) Survey conducted in 1993/94, there are 778 formal food processing industries. There are also many informal businesses. In the small-scale food processing industrial sector, bakeries have the highest number, followed by food manufacturing and dairy products. The central development region has the largest number of food processing industries followed by the eastern region. The production from such industries includes dairy products, preserved fruits and vegetables, bakery products, cocoa and confectionery and other food products. Most of the large- and medium-scale food processing industries use imported diesel and petrol, while large quantities of fuel wood is used by small-scale bakeries and sweetmeat or tea shops.

Women's involvement is sought in food processing activities, as they are the ones who produce food for their families. Women process food not only for immediate household consumption but also to preserve it for a longer duration (for off-season supply and sale). This does not mean that women are experts in the production of food on a large scale, but they do have local knowledge and expertise to produce, mostly at household scale. Enterprise development in food processing is not easy, and requires careful planning and management of various aspects of processing including the choice and use of energy and related technologies, so that the product will be hygienic and accepted in the market. For this kind of production and management, training is needed for the producers in food processing, business and management skills. These abilities will build up the confidence and expertise of these women.

Centre for Rural Technology (CRT)

CRT is a non-governmental private sector organization, established in 1989. It is engaged in developing and promoting technologies which are effective in meeting the basic needs of the rural population and improving their support systems. It believes that such technologies should be widely promoted and employed to help reduce human drudgery, to alleviate poverty and to contribute to equitable and environmentally sensitive sustainable development. In this context, the centre plays a catalytic role in assisting the government, non-government organizations, research institutions and technology production centres in developing and delivering technology packages to rural communities. CRT has been actively engaged in upgrading traditional technologies and developing new technologies. It promotes and disseminates technologies that emphasize the maximum use of local resources in dealing with rural needs, and contributes towards the empowerment of rural communities.

Identifying the needs of women in food processing enterprises

Visits to women food processing entrepreneurs reveal several problems: the availability of packaging materials and bottles; marketing of the product which relies solely on small shops or friends and relatives; competition from imported products with good promotion and attractive packaging, and competition from local small-scale processors. Since traditional energy is needed in such food processing activities, the price of energy affects the costs of production. As the energy price has nearly doubled in the last few years, entrepreneurs have to increase the price of their products, which means that people of low income cannot afford to buy them. Again, they have to compete with imported products.

Both the hygiene and quality of products, and suited to consumer's taste and choice, have to be maintained for marketing. Small-scale entrepreneurs cannot afford to pay much attention to these matters, however: they are dependent upon household equipment and energy technologies which sometimes contaminate food.

A lack of self-confidence was found to be one of the major problems faced by women entrepreneurs which hindered the scope for their business (see box describing 'A business failure'). This was a result of being brought up in and dependent on a male-dominated society where fathers, brothers and husbands take responsibility for all management tasks.

A lack of capital and biased attitudes from administrators and bank officials are another problem for women wanting to obtain credit to start a business. Because of prejudices against women, they have to take loans from other sources with high interest rates. However, some organizations (Small Farmer Development, Micro Credit Project for Rural Women) have set priorities to provide loans to women in rural areas under a group collateral system. The programmes have not yet spread widely to cover the large number of needy women entrepreneurs.

> **A business failure**
>
> *Dalmoth* (a snack made from a mixture of fried mung, peanuts and soya beans) looked like a ray of hope for Bel Maya, who was desperately looking for a solution to her financial problems. According to many of her friends who were in the *dalmoth* trade, it was 'good business': easy to prepare, pack and sell. Bel Maya is an illiterate housewife who did not have an opportunity to be trained for self-employment. She had to depend on her husband's small salary as a government servant, which he brought home once a month. Naturally, life was a battle for her and the family.
>
> Bel Maya decided to try her luck producing *dalmoth*. However, her lack of confidence prevented her from actively engaging in the business from the beginning. Purchasing material and handling cash were done by her husband. When it came to marketing, they had to depend on the same shops that were already selling *dalmoth*. These agreed to accept her product since she had used the best-quality vegetable oil for frying, but the profit margin was very low and some other sales outlets had to be sought.
>
> Bel Maya needed training but was intimidated because of her lack of education. Quite a few batches of burnt black mung were thrown away. She learnt by experience that the mung had to be fried first and then the peanuts. Unaware of the existence of energy-saving cooking stoves, she used a kerosene stove for frying *dalmoth*. Raw materials were purchased in small quantities as they could not invest large sums of money to buy at wholesale rates. Frequent price fluctuations badly affected their business, as they could not revise the product price accordingly. They were now selling to neighbours and relatives, who hardly realized the complex marketing issues. Making things worse, Bel Maya's mild nature was misused by her customers: they often took *dalmoth* on a 'buy now, pay later' basis and then payments were conveniently forgotten. They have not maintained any records of their initial investments. Calculations were made by her husband, and there is no visible improvement in the financial or social conditions of her family, although they started the venture two years ago. The reasons for her failure can be listed as a lack of self-confidence and of training in technical and business skills.

Thus motivation and training in these areas are needed so that women can increase their confidence. Furthermore, awareness raising is needed for their male counterparts to remove their prejudices against women and to make them understand that women have the ability and can manage the enterprise more profitably if they are given opportunities and responsibility.

Training in food processing and business management are needed in order to ensure quality and hygiene in food processing, and the selection of the most appropriate technologies. The training should be an all-round package of enterprise development, ranging from the planning of raw materials, to processing techniques to financial management and marketing.

Issues affecting the training of small-scale food processors

Education. Education and literacy play an important part in creating awareness for new ventures and acquiring information, but in Nepal, only 25 per cent of women are literate in the whole of the country and only 15 per cent in rural areas.

Male-dominated society. In Nepal, society is dominated by males and women are largely ignored during the dissemination of information. Without any information or technological know-how, women are generally just passive recipients of technology. Thus they can become confused and hesitant in adopting such technologies and it is difficult to bring about change in their preconceived ideas.

A Nepalese success story

Ratna Lama's day begins early in the morning. After attending to the family breakfast, she works in her small fruit garden or gives her husband a 'helping hand' on their farm. Her work there normally includes weeding, preparing the vegetable beds for the next crop and, during harvest time, collecting the harvest. Having toiled until late afternoon, she comes home with some vegetables, not forgetting some grass for the goat. Although other chores, such as preparing the midday meal, bringing water and tidying up the house, take most of her time, she manages to find some leisure hours during the day!

The Lama family could hardly make ends meet. Their farm and garden did not give them adequate money even for the children's basic needs. Ratna's lack of education and her other obligations prevented her from going out to find employment elsewhere. Ratna tried her hand at sun-drying *karela* (bitter gourd) and making *amot* (a mango candy). The traditional methods gave her poor results although the family welcomed it. Birds and other animals took her dried produce, and that which remained was covered with dust and were dirty. Moreover, it had an unpleasant black colour, which stopped her from selling the produce to outsiders. Her efforts gave the family some fruits and vegetables during the off season, but no money.

Ratna met the US Save the Children branch officers on her way to the market to get ideas for overcoming the problems of her venture. They told her of the existence of a solar dryer, which simply works with the freely available sunlight. She needed training, but Save the Children agreed to pay the training costs. She was able to come to the Centre for Rural Technology, where she was trained to operate and maintain the solar dryer. Making use of her hard-earned savings, she invested Rs2000 in the solar dryer. She took time to learn to use and maintain it by herself. At first, she did not worry about the markets. Not knowing how well her products would do, she first sold her *amot* and *karela* to the neighbours, who liked them. She had five regular customers at first. The number increased, while the persevering woman tried to improve the product quality.

She was already confident with the operation of the dryer and discovered that losses were minimal. No birds took her *amot* and it looked clean. The colour of the finished product was attractive. She bought polythene bags of different sizes, packed the products and sealed them with the help of a lighted candle. When more of the fresh produce (and of course, the time to process it) is available, she sells the products at the 'hat bazaar' which she can reach in 15 minutes.

She sells about 24kg of dried *karela* and 1.5kg of *amot* a year, making use of the little free time she gets during the day. Her raw materials are from the garden and the farm. At the moment, she earns about Rs3600 a year which makes a good contribution towards her family budget. Exercise books and pencils needed by the children do not worry her as much as they did five years ago. She limits her food business to her spare time, but she intends to expand her business by purchasing another machine and employing some people from the locality.

Training facilities in the food processing sector. There are a number of institutions, such as the department of Cottage and Village Industries and the Food Research Laboratory already conducting training courses on food processing. However, the output of these institutions has not been able to meet the demand. NGOs or private co-operative sector institutions who have contacts and linkages with grassroot communities should develop training programmes for micro food processing enterprises.

Quality. Hygiene and quality control are major factors in the food processing sector in Nepal. By following simple rules of hygiene, the products of microenterprises and small businesses could be greatly improved (see box describing 'A Nepalese success story').

Food processing technologies and machinery. The lack of food processing technologies and supplies of machinery is another problem. Some equipment is manufactured locally but it is too costly to obtain, particularly by poorer entrepreneurs. Most equipment is imported from India.

Investment capital and credit facilities. Poor entrepreneurs are faced with problems such as a lack of investment capital and credit facilities. Credit on reasonable terms should be linked to the purchase of equipment and establishment of the microfood processing activities.

Packaging and storage. The available packaging materials are imported from India which is costly for the small-scale processor.

Co-ordination. There are several support organizations that cater specifically for women, but a lack of co-ordination between them, absence of well thought-out strategies and a lack of commitment to tie up human and material resources have reduced the level of support they provide.

With technical and financial assistance from UNDP/UNIDO, the Women Entrepreneurs' Association of Nepal has started to support women in several areas of economic activities. The duration of training varies according to the requirements and contents of the course. In general, training programmes of six months, three months, one month and one week are organized.

During the training conducted so far by various organizations, the following food products were identified as useful for production at the small scale: pickles, chutney, sauces, fruit juices, potato chips, traditional dehydrated food products (*tituaa* and *maseura*), *gundruk*, *sinhi*, fruit candies (*laspi*, *kuvindo*, ginger), fermented beverages (wine, cider and brandy), dried mushrooms, cereal flakes such as *chiura*, beaten cereals and flakes, bread, cookies, noodles, snack products, spices and aromatic herbs, medicinal herbs, ice cream, yoghurt, cheese and condensed milk.

Lessons and recommendations

Training should include technology, business management and record keeping as well as marketing aspects of food production. After a simple management course, women should be encouraged or assisted to choose the product they want to produce, then be involved in the food processing skills training along with marketing and quality production.

A trained woman can run her business smoothly whilst one lacking proper training may experience many difficulties. Training is necessary for success in any business. A microenterprise in food processing and drying can be suitable for women in both urban and rural areas. Some products are locally marketed in town centres and some can be transported to urban areas. Microenterprises increase the economic empowerment of women, which ultimately helps the well-being of the family, and begins to combat the vicious circle of poverty.

In order to prevent confusion, there should be simple, clear and detailed information with illustrations on what the food processing devices do, how they work, and how to use, repair and maintain them.

The two stories presented in boxes illustrate the value of training in establishing a successful small-scale business.

Training in food processing technologies in Peru

CARMEN RODRIGUEZ, DIANA COLQUICHAGUA, DANIEL RODRIGUEZ, PIM HEIJSTER and WALTER RIOS

Introduction

Peru, in the central part of the west coast of South America, has three main climatic zones: the dry coastal strip; the mountainous Andes and the tropical Amazon basin. It has diverse and important agricultural resources which promise great agro-industrial opportunities. Although the last decade has included some years of economic instability and social disorder, the country is now on the road to recovery. This situation favours training activities in the agro-processing sector as more people seek to become part of a productive system as a means of obtaining employment and improving their incomes.

For 12 years, Intermediate Technology (IT Peru) has been developing activities in food processing through training and technical assistance to small producers in the capital, Lima, and the provinces. At the same time, it has been working on the implementation and adaptation of technologies appropriate for small productive units. From 1989 to 1991, IT Peru participated in the implementation of the project 'Technological food processing alternatives in three areas of Peru', which was funded by the United Nations Fund for Women. This project was based in three training centres, one in each of the three major climatic zones, and aimed to improve employment and income generating opportunities for women. The experience gained in this project, which included several market surveys and investigations in Lima, Pucallpa and Huancayo, permitted IT Peru to identify and develop 10 different technologies and over 35 specific products. In 1992, two pilot courses were carried out

Traditional food products in Peru (IT/Janet Boston)

jointly by IT Peru and INPET (Institute for the Promotion of Participative Development) to assist in the preparation of the 'Small-scale food processing training facility project in Peru'. This was approved and co-financed by the Overseas Development Administration (now DFID, Department for International Development), European Commission (EC) and the CODESPA Foundation from Spain, for a period of five years.

Developing the training course

Objective. The objective of the training was to encourage employment, to increase incomes and to promote the economic development of low-income sectors in Peru by means of small food processing enterprises.

Partners. IT Peru implemented the training course in collaboration with INPET and the National Industrial Training Service (SENATI). INPET, a non-governmental organization specializing in management training and assistance, was responsible for providing the co-ordination and materials and for giving training on management topics for the courses. SENATI, a semi-private organization contributed to the training, skills improvement and advanced training of workers in productive activities. IT Peru developed and delivered the technical components of the programme.

Needs assessment. An in-depth needs assessment was carried out through discussions with people involved in small-scale food processing, including agencies active in the areas. This identified the specific training needs of different beneficiary groups, the availability of training and suitable facilities, and the existence of food processing activities.

Course preparation. In order to prepare the training courses, a series of activities were undertaken:

o Technical development work was carried out in key areas in order to develop appropriate technology packages for different products and identify equipment. A good example is the development of a small-scale ice-cream making machine.
o IT Peru carried out several market studies and surveys. These ranged from product specific studies to regional investigations. Rapid feasibility studies were carried out, together with investigations into product and commodity prices.
o A range of technical papers, educational materials and methodology guides were prepared to help trainers organize courses clearly and effectively.
o Monitoring and evaluation is essential to show that the training is effective and to be able to improve the courses continually. An elaborate system was established with post course assessment and field visits to participants after the courses.
o During follow-up visits, participants received individual technical support in their place of work.

Course structure and contents

The total duration of a course is from 18 to 30 hours with an average of 15 to 20 participants. The courses consist of two parts: the technology component (which accounts for 70 per cent of the time) and the management component (which accounts for 30 per cent). Figure 9.1 shows the general outline of the course structure, which is modified according to the type of participants, their needs and the geographical area.

```
Training course structure

1st module
Welcome
Presentation of technology
Description of processing flow
Practical demonstration

2nd module
Marketing aspects
Group formation
Practical production

3rd module
Final product quality control
Evaluation of the results
Determination of the sale price
```

Figure 9.1 *General outline of course structure*

The first module is designed to break down barriers, establish a dialogue amongst the participants and to overcome distrust which is often evident amongst a group of women. Sharing individual experiences with other participants has been found to be an excellent means of bringing the group together. The use of slides, videos and flow charts (an example of which is given in Figure 9.2) improves the participants' attention and

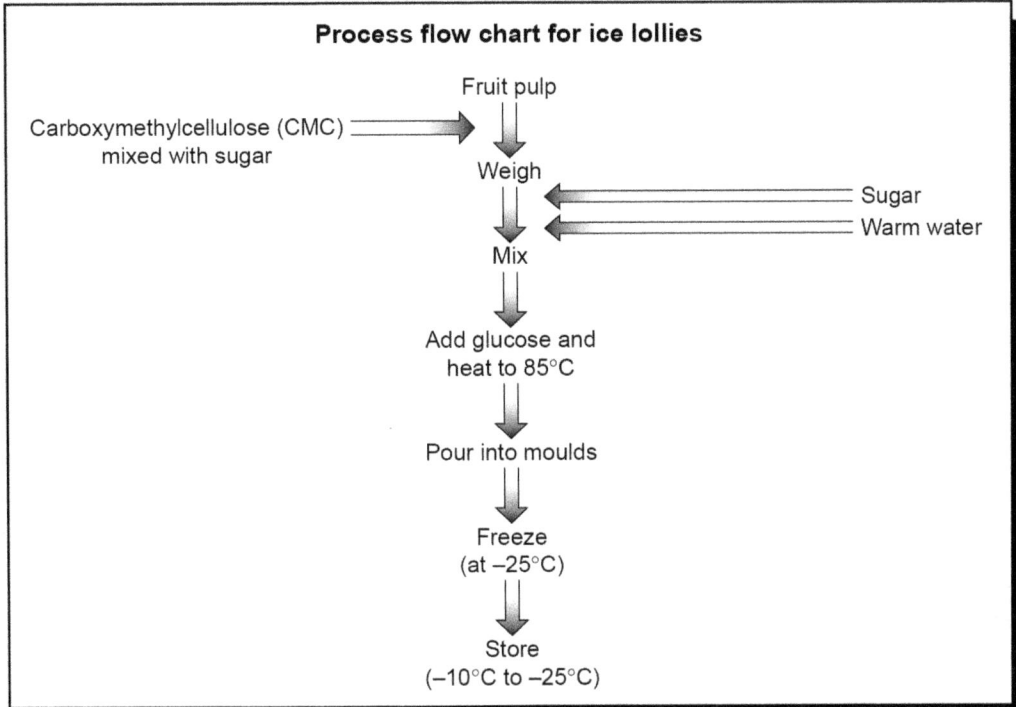

Figure 9.2 *Ice-lolly production flow diagram*

interest. The participants were given all the written materials during the first session so that they could easily follow the different aspects of the course, more easily understand demonstrations and familiarize themselves with the production processes. At the end of this module the trainer gives a practical demonstration of how to make the product.

The second module begins with marketing, in which the results of market studies and surveys are presented to the participants. These provide up-to-date information on opportunities for introducing or improving their products. This is complemented with exercises in which groups of four to five participants have to find solutions to specific marketing problems. Then, small groups of participants make the product under the supervision of several technicians. This part of the course is generally quite motivating and develops the participants' skills. Many of the practical training sessions are carried out in local commercial bakeries and dairies. This enables the participants to watch a profit-making business in action and to discuss the opportunities and constraints with successful entrepreneurs.

In the third module, the manufactured products are evaluated by group members. Particular attention is paid to aspects related to quality control, hygiene and equipment handling. In addition, the costs and sales price are determined from the price of raw materials, inputs and services available in the area.

Individual follow-up, as a part of post-course evaluation, has been of great help to the course organizers and has allowed better selection of participants. IT Peru has been able to organize appropriate training courses and also offer timely technical assistance in collaboration with institutions sharing common goals. At present, 16 per cent of the total number of participants have required technical assistance after the training.

Project impact

An external evaluation carried out in 1996 showed that 809 people had been trained (35 per cent men and 65 per cent women).

start some new food processing units and has reinforced the activity of many existing units.

One of the positive impacts of the course is the way technical improvements allow microentrepreneurs to increase their market and income and, consequently, facilitates their access to other markets. Increasing privatization and unemployment in Peru has created the need for self-employment, and food processing is an attractive, appropriate activity.

Impact on women's groups
The evaluation has shown that:

o 60 per cent have used the technologies they learned;
o 12 per cent have improved their existing production;
o 7 per cent have begun production to generate income;
o 40 per cent have learned how to contribute to improvement of survival strategies;
o 4 per cent have carried out production for home consumption; and
o 13 per cent plan to start production.

Training uses locally available materials and equipment (IT/R Velachaga)

Of those trained, 50 per cent are microentrepreneurs, 36 per cent extension workers and 14 per cent come from women's groups.

Impact on microentrepreneurs
The evaluation showed that:

o 9 per cent of the people trained had become microentrepreneurs;
o 19 per cent reinforced their existing production by increasing sales and/or improving product quality;
o 15 per cent had been able to formalize and register their businesses;
o 18 per cent had begun to establish an enterprise or planned to do so; and
o 60 per cent had acquired knowledge but had yet to put it into practice.

These results, although they are lower than initially expected, have been increasing every year. The training programme has helped

The most popular technologies are those requiring minimum investment and which involve simple technologies. Women have adopted these technologies and have started to generate incomes, establish new roles in the family and consequently, to gain a greater degree of independence. Production by these beneficiaries is at levels that do not allow them access to large markets. However, their products give them an average monthly income of between 200 and 250 soles (US$75–94). The training has been very important for these women, since it makes them more aware of their position and surroundings. We have observed an increase in the self-esteem and self-valuation of these poor women, many of whom have had little education.

The impact on extension workers and instructors
A total of 290 instructors from technical and educational institutions have been trained. The evaluation indicated that:

o 53 per cent have included the material learnt in their instruction programmes;
o 9 per cent have used this material to complement their courses;
o 38 per cent acquired knowledge which they have been unable to use in their work, due to the lack of infrastructure and implementation materials.

In the long term, the economic benefits of training trainers can be seen as the extension workers pass on their skills and knowledge to other trainees (see box describing the experience of Miss Gomez). One of the most beneficial aspects of training fieldworkers and extension workers is the multiplier effect on the cost-benefit ratio. The training courses have permitted the participants to be better informed, to update their knowledge and improve their methods of teaching.

Making candy is a popular techology for training (Alberta Higa)

The most popular technologies for training

The courses on ice-cream production, including the production of ice cream on a

> **Miss Yolanda Gomez Acero – teaching small business people**
>
> Miss Gomez is a teacher at the Superior Technological Institute SAUSA at Jauja, attended by about 60 students per year. She has participated in four IT Peru training courses: chocolate, ice-cream, marshmallows and sweet gum production. She teaches chocolate preparation because the school has its own equipment. In the case of ice-creams, she teaches in a place where the school is able to rent equipment. Marshmallow production was taught only once, as the necessary equipment is not available. Miss Gomez teaches everything related to the methodology of food processing, management aspects and also holds practical classes. At present, 5 per cent of her students are using the equipment at the institute to produce and sell their products privately. The institute permits the students free access to these facilities, but only from Monday to Friday. She considers that in the future, about 70 per cent of her students will start a small food business, a further 25 per cent will be employed by a company and the remaining 5 per cent will study at the university.

> **Mr Emilio Cabezas Cueva – expanding an ice-cream business**
>
> Mr Cabezas is 40 years old and has four children of school age. Before attending the IT Peru courses, he had been producing ice-cream during the summer months. He says that after attending three courses and receiving technical assistance from IT Peru he could increase his production and improve his product by using new ingredients, and he could also lower the cost in some cases. He introduced two flavours and he admits that although he had been using pasteurized milk and boiled water before attending the IT Peru courses, he now takes more care over hygiene and product-handling aspects. At present, he produces fruit and milk ice-creams and hires two or three full-time workers in addition to 20 people working in marketing. He had to increase his installed capacity by 10 per cent. As a result, he increased his sales by 30 per cent and his net profits by 20 per cent. He calculates that the growth of his business is due to IT Peru's training and technical assistance, which he received without any cost.

stick and yoghurt and fruit ice creams, proved to be of greatest interest to microentrepreneurs from Lima and Huancayo. To date they represent almost a quarter of the total number of courses. The second most popular product was chocolate. This course was targeted mainly at women, extension workers and microentrepreneurs in the three areas in the project. Other courses dealt with the preparation of pickles, fruit squashes, fruit spirits, yoghurt, marshmallows, sweet gums, wines, snacks, bread and pastry, sweet bread, milled products and quality control.

Sustainability

One of the objectives of the project was for the courses to become self-financing through participants' fees. This has not yet been achieved. Only 3 per cent of the total costs have been recovered due to the low income of the participants. It is essential to have a strategy for ensuring the sustainability and transference of the training programme, and the project continues to work towards this goal.

SENATI has now taken responsibility for continuing the work and replicating it on a larger scale through 33 training centres throughout the country. In the past, SENATI only had experience in bread and pastry production, but since its participation in the project, it has broadened its product range.

Lessons learnt

Adaptability. The most important lesson learnt is the importance of adaptability: the adaptability of the instructors to work in rural areas; the adaptability of small local manufacturers to produce food processing equipment at a cost (US$200–$3800) which the microentrepreneurs and small business people can afford; the adaptability of the follow-up system to obtain information about the participants' knowledge and expectations; and also the technical assistance to provide the participants with technical, management or information support after completion of the training.

Participant selection. A better selection of participants has increased the course effectiveness, ensuring that only people committed to training and food processing participate in the course. This can be seen by the steady and progressive improvement in the impact of the courses.

Collaboration and co-ordination. IT Peru has learnt the need for a close co-operation and co-ordination with other local institutions so that they can carry out similar or complementary activities to those of the project in order to optimize efforts and to increase the impact of the project. It is important to strengthen communications among institutions committed to the design and promotion of the courses. The co-ordination of non-financial services must be included.

Information. The fact that IT Peru has access to international information sources, and knowing the microenterprises' needs has enabled the project to design and manufacture the equipment which could improve the quality of the products, thus making them more marketable.

Monitoring. It is essential to carry out the monitoring immediately after each course in order to identify needs, provide technical assistance services and improve the training provided.

Further reading

1. 'Training in food processing technology, Peru', Alcazar, Manuel and Tomasi, Scott (1996), CODESPA, Spain.
2. 'Necessidades actuales de capacitacion en technologias de alimentos y gestion empresarial' (1994), IT Peru.

Fruit processing training in South Africa

JOYENE ISAACS, LAETITIA MOGGEE and PHILLIP C. FOURIE

Introduction

South Africa is a country of contrasts, where a small proportion of the inhabitants have had access to land, finance and information while the majority were denied the most basic rights. With the change in government and democratization, the previously disadvantaged suddenly gained opportunities through policy changes. Organizations changed their operational framework to accommodate these needs and to facilitate the transfer of technology and information. INFRUITEC is one of the organizations that has adopted a changed mission to ensure disadvantaged communities access to the technology of the past 40 years.

INFRUITEC is one of 16 institutes of the Agricultural Research Council and specializes in deciduous fruit (and alternative crops) research and technology development. The Processing Technology Division specializes in developing low-technology processing techniques for resource-limited farmers and devotes a considerable amount of time to the transfer of technology to these communities. INFRUITEC has established a new structure, FIRS (Fruit Information and Research Service), to assist with information and technology for fruit production opportunities, new skills and economic

Drying fruits is part of the INFRUITEC course (ARC-INFRUITEC)

agricultural opportunities to disadvantaged farmers. Several agricultural priorities, especially cultivation and processing of fruit, were identified by different communities using participatory rural appraisal (PRA).

Poverty in rural areas has risen sharply over the last decade, with people migrating to the urban sector. Unemployment has exacerbated the poor conditions and added to people's inability to plan and implement strategies to improve rural livelihoods. The lack of education, access to land and water as well as information and technology ensures that rural people are trapped in a poverty cycle, with no immediate end in sight.

Resource-limited communities often lack the skills, practical experience and knowledge of technology to add value to their products. Technology transfer in processing techniques enables farmers and entrepreneurs to gain additional skills and add value to their products. Through this initiative they can increase their income and create job opportunities for unemployed community members. Through interaction and participation, FIRS strives to redress the constraints experienced by rural communities. Processing training is not done in isolation, but forms part of an overall fruit production strategy, where an improved range of fruit (i.e. alternative crops) and value-adding skills are addressed.

Target groups

The FIRS team works in communities having different environmental conditions, poverty levels, educational attainments and land tenure. The communities are in the following locations: Western Cape; Haarlem, Buysplaas, Jamestown and townships within the Cape Metropole and the Northern Cape; Kheis, Klipfontein, Steinkopf and Spoegrivier.

This case study deals with communities within Western Cape Province, of Haarlem and Buysplaas. Haarlem is situated in the Langkloof in the Southern Cape. The main sources of income are subsistence farming, seasonal employment on adjacent commercial farms, state pensions and small-scale hawking of fruit bought from the surrounding commercial farms. Among the population of three to four thousand are many farmers with good agricultural skills and knowledge of vegetables and deciduous fruit.

In each community, there is a responsible person selected by the community to facilitate training courses, meetings, workshops and the general flow of information. FIRS informs the different communities about training opportunities and, through community meetings, persons are selected to attend these training courses. To facilitate a flow of information and technology, an invitation to each community requests a set number of participants (three to four) to attend, but no other criteria are suggested.

Only ten persons are invited to attend each training course, which can accommodate illiterate or functionally literate persons. People who have participated in the training course have included teachers, housewives, farmers and teenagers. With the technical and developmental experience of the trainers, the course can be adapted for farmers, rural animation officers and extension officers. Each decentralized training course is tailor-made for the participants and will be adapted for illiterate persons where necessary.

Outline of the training course

A fruit processing training course for trainers working in resource-limited communities was held at the Montagu Training Centre in the Western Cape. Six trainers participated in the five-day training course held in January 1997; three from Haarlem, two from Mosselbay and one from Buysplaas. As an introduction and to break the ice, we halved three different kinds of fruit and each participant had to select a fruit piece. Participants had to find their partner or other half; then find out more about one another for approximately five minutes. Participants then had the opportunity to tell the larger group about their partner.

After the introduction, a needs assessment as well as participants' expectations and fears were discussed. Each participant was given three cards to write down their needs, expectations and fears and these were displayed on news print for the duration of the course, and also used during the evaluation at the end of the course. Each participant received a manual with all the information on the different processes that were to be demonstrated, as well as recipes. Short lectures were given on each processing technique, which was also demonstrated. Lectures were accompanied by videos, slides and visual drawings for better understanding and were presented in the official language of the participants so that trainers did not need interpreters.

Participants were introduced to building of drying racks by means of a demonstration and then they had to build their own in groups of two. This exercise assisted them to settle in and to feel more comfortable working as a team. The preparation of fruit for different sulphuring techniques was done after the teams had evaluated their co-participants' drying racks. The entire process from harvesting the fruit to sulphuring was demonstrated. After preparation of the fruit, the different sulphuring techniques were practised and fruits were left in the sun for two days and then stacked to dry in the wind.

On the second day, hygiene aspects were addressed by way of a lecture and by using the previous day's experience to cross-check hygienic practices. Participants realized that they had not washed their hands or the fruit or even the drying racks before starting with the preparation of the fruit. Participants were introduced to making fruit leathers and practised this technique after the preparation of the fruit was demonstrated. Each made his own fruit leather.

On the third day we started jam-making by asking the participants who had experience of cooking jam to share their methods with the others. Acknowledging and using the local indigenous knowledge of participants improved the relationship between participants and trainers. The trainers' methods and their practical demonstrations were improved by the contributions of the participants. After a demonstration, groups of two prepared their jam by different methods to investigate the effects on colour and quality, of different techniques, especially overcooking.

After a chutney-making demonstration, each group made their own chutney. To relax and socialize, the afternoon was used to show participants around the Montagu district. Participants were taken to a farm where apricots are dried on a commercial scale. A barbecue was organized for the evening to establish firm links between community members and INFRUITEC. An evaluation at the end of the course was done by referring to the cards the delegates had written at the beginning of the course, noting fears and expectations. We discussed whether the course had succeeded in allaying their fears and accommodating their expectations. We also used evaluation forms to assess the different sections (i.e. the lectures, practical demonstrations and accommodation). Each participant received an attendance certificate and the products they had made during the course.

Further evaluation and inspections were carried out by visiting participants three months later in their respective communities to investigate their processing activity. Other women from these communities who were interested were invited to join the community workshop. We gave a demonstration of making fruit candies, and handed each delegate from the community a written copy of the method. We inspected all the products that participants had made and discussed the follow-up workshops they held with community members after the training. A number of people in the different communities are interested in processing products such as fruit candies, but specific problems need addressing: for example, some equipment is expensive and financial support would need to be found.

Practical sessions are essential for effective learning (ARC-INFRUITEC)

Facilities

The Montagu Training Centre is a basic building with no elaborate facilities for processing training. There are a few lecture rooms, a large hall, and a small kitchen. A hostel is connected to the main building where the participants were accommodated.

INFRUITEC trainers used training materials that could be transported from one community to the next. Equipment such as gas stoves, knives and spoons were bought for the training course (communities often have no electricity but gas is readily available in rural areas). Participants could therefore associate themselves with the training environment and be more comfortable in these circumstances.

Successes and problems

Excellent feedback was received from the participants during evaluations and recommendations will be utilized to improve future courses. Some of the participants have already commenced training other people in their communities. They have also prepared many products for marketing and cannot keep ahead of the demand. Follow-up visits will be made after the course to all the participants to give them assistance with training other members of their respective communities. The course proved that there is a great need for the local population to be trained to do their own processing and we are planning to extend this course to other regions. A follow-up evaluation in the communities was made by INFRUITEC trainers to assess the successes and problems with the training course.

Successes

- INFRUITEC's involvement in transferring technology to disadvantaged communities.
- The use of participatory rural appraisal (PRA) techniques to conduct needs assessment before the start of the training course.
- Some participants started workshops to train other members in fruit processing techniques.
- The visual training materials complemented technology transfer to diversified target groups.
- Some participants are using newly learned skills to expand their economic activities to raise income.
- Gas stoves were used successfully because of the unavailability of electricity.

Problems

- The target groups are not uniform (in terms of literacy, experience and confidence levels) so the course has to cater for

- all participants, which makes it difficult to gauge participant's understanding.
- The availability of materials (bottles, fruit out of season and ingredients) is a limiting factor for community members.
- We did not have cold storage facilities and had a problem with overripe fruit due to ambient storage.
- Participants had to leave their part-time jobs on the farms to attend the course and their participation meant a loss of income for their families. However, payment to participants would lead to an increase in applications for training courses and would not provide an acceptable solution. Participants would not necessarily be potential fruit processing entrepreneurs but people in need of the finance.
- Although good-quality products are produced, the lack of marketing skills to promote their own products limits their hope of achieving success.
- Although participants are very keen to start processing, a lack of finance to pursue their own small-scale business is a major constraint.
- Although we were lucky to have a group with which we could communicate, language problems can occur and the help of interpreters may be needed.
- During fruit drying training, sunny weather is needed but does not always occur, and this can obstruct the progress of the training course.

Lessons learnt

Several important lessons have been learnt from this training programme. The feedback from evaluations and follow-up in the field is being used constructively to improve the course for future trainees. Some of the more pertinent lessons learnt are highlighted below:

- Through using PRA methodologies, participants relaxed and learnt more processing techniques.
- Practical demonstrations enhanced the learning curve of participants, but the short lecture strengthened their grasp of the technology.
- The course design facilitated team work and the sharing of local indigenous knowledge.
- The evaluation at the end of the course gave trainers useful insights for future courses and designs to accommodate different target groups.
- The size of the group should not exceed ten persons, because attention to individuals is important in a diverse group.
- The processing training must use locally available fruit.
- Within this course design illiterate persons were accommodated.

It is envisaged that, with the evaluation comments received from trainees and, based on these important lessons learnt, the IN-FRUITEC training course will continue to expand and to improve to meet the needs of the participants.

11
Food processing training in Sri Lanka
VISHAKA HIDELLAGE

Introduction

There are dusty roads, golden fields and hundreds of rural people walking barefoot under the hot sun, carrying baskets filled with their produce. Others ride their bicycles from morning to night, selling their produce in neighbouring villages or nearby towns. These are Sri Lanka's entrepreneurs, struggling to run their businesses and solve the problems of lack of money, scarcity of raw materials and marketing inexperience. Some of them are born entrepreneurs, others are not. All of them could benefit from training.

Sri Lanka is a country with a predominantly agricultural economy, despite attempts during the last two decades to promote industrial development. Agro-processing therefore plays an essential role in making the lives of poor people better, by increasing their incomes and creating employment opportunities. Many agro-processing businesses produce only subsistence incomes for poor families, and during the agricultural season these businesses are closed as extra labour is needed in the field. The business owner either cannot afford to hire or is unable to find workers. Therefore profitability of the businesses in conventional terms is low. The poor image and assumed low profitability mean that it is very difficult to access support services or facilities for such businesses. Small-scale food processing businesses are therefore

Sri Lanka is a country with a predominantly agricultural economy (IT)

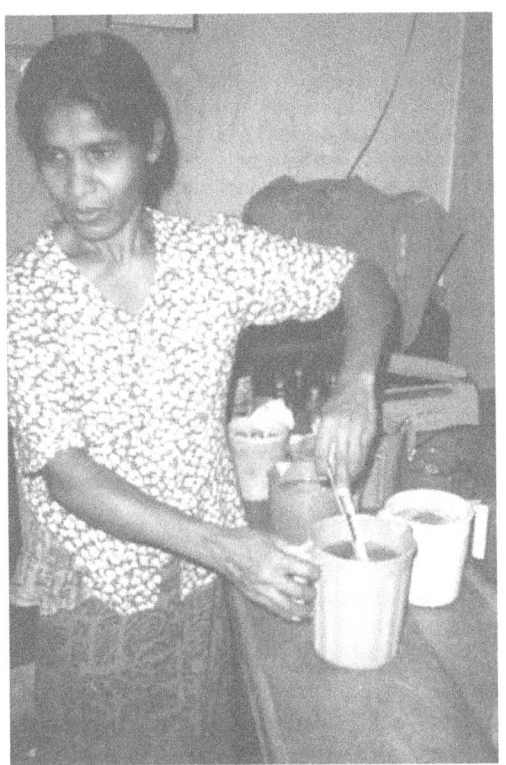

Sweet making in Sri Lanka (IT/Ann Watts)

considered to be unprofitable and unsuccessful by the policy- and decision-makers.

The agro-processing programme of Intermediate Technology (IT) started its training at a time when the only formal training in food processing was available at post-graduate level. The larger-scale enterprises could get advice from government institutions, such as the Ceylon Institute of Scientific and Industrial Research and the Industrial Development Board. However, these organizations were not geared to cater for small-scale enterprises. In 1987, IT established a food processing training course specifically for small-scale women entrepreneurs. The course was developed into a training of trainers course in 1989 to increase the number of rural entrepreneurs who could benefit. The courses were held at various locations from 1987–91. Of all the institutions at which the course was held, the International Centre for the Training of Rural Leaders (ICTRL), situated in a serene location in Yodhagama, Embilipitiya, was considered the most appropriate.

The training facility was set up in Embilipitiya, within the key training centre for leadership skills development. Approximately 5000 rural leaders are trained in the centre each year and they pass on what they learn about the small food processing sector to interested people in their villages.

Demand for training grew and IT realized that this could not be met through the annual training of trainers course alone. There was a need for a training facility which could cater for the training needs of the small-scale food processing sector throughout the year. Discussions were held with ICTRL and the Ministry of Policy Planning and Implementation to create a training facility in food processing within ICTRL. In 1991, the Cathy Rich Memorial Food Processing Training Unit (CRMFPTU) was established. The training unit is named after Cathy Rich, an IT food technologist who worked in Sri Lanka and sadly met with a road accident there and died. The interest from a memorial fund set up by her parents subsidizes the annual training of trainers course.

The training programme

The objective of the training programme is to enable poor people engaged in food processing microenterprises and small-scale

> **Training of trainers' course content**
>
> *Phase I: Introduction to the training* (duration – 1 week)
> *Subject areas.* The role of a trainer, participatory techniques in development, market feasibility for small businesses, recognizing an entrepreneur, developing an action plan, introduction to food technology and appropriate equipment and identifying resources at village level.
>   This module allows participants to decide whether to proceed with the second and third phases. The trainees are sent to their project locations after the first week for one month and the trainers visit them in the field and help them solve the problems they face. Therefore, it can be described as the 'screening phase' to identify active participants.
>
> *Phase II: Food-based enterprises* (duration – 2 weeks)
> *Subject areas.* Sharing of field experiences; project proposals; basics of food technology; practical sessions on food technology and designing a training course.
>   Trainees are released to the field to share their knowledge with their beneficiaries and asked to identify entrepreneurs and potential food enterprises. They are given the responsibility to identify training needs and conduct training.
>
> *Phase III: Business development* (duration – 2 weeks)
> *Subject areas.* Problems and issues – sharing experiences; financial management; project management; entrepreneurship development; communications skills, public relations and designing a training course.
>   Refresher workshops are held to provide support to the fieldworkers and to update their skills.

businesses, to develop skills and increase their access to information, which will contribute towards gaining better control over their lives and their communities. This will be achieved by increasing the number and profitability of small-scale food processing businesses in Sri Lanka and in the region and thereby stimulating rural employment, self sufficiency and entrepreneurial activity. The types of training offered by the centre differ according to the needs of the participants.

Annual training of trainers course. This course is a combination of business development and food technology with a mixture of classroom sessions and field work (see box describing course content). It is a residential course, of five weeks, conducted in three phases with intervals to allow the trainees to use the knowledge gained in their work. The training of trainers course is now conducted in two languages – Sinhala and Tamil – to make it more accessible to a wider audience.

Short courses on a specific technology or product area. These courses are conducted for small-scale entrepreneurs and the training package is specifically designed to suit the requirements of the requesting organizations or entrepreneurs.

One-day training. Small-scale entrepreneurs also have direct access to resources and services available at the training unit, through one-day courses which focus on specific technological processes and products. These courses have recently been modified to make them more affordable for small-scale entrepreneurs. Training is mainly carried out 'in-house' by trained staff of the CRMFPTU, which greatly reduces the cost.

Regional training programme. This workshop offers training in small-scale food processing for extension workers or officials who can support grassroots development

Year	Cathy Rich		Refreshers		Bakery		Confectionery		Fruit processing		One-day	
	Courses	Trainers	Courses	Trainers	Courses	Trainers	Courses	Trainers	Courses	Trainers	Courses	Trainers
1992	1	8	2	7	1	8	1	5	–	–	–	–
1993	1	8	3	18	–	–	–	–	–	–	8	67
1994	1	9	–	–	2	25	2	15	–	–	3	10
1995	1	13	–	–	1	9	–	–	1	12	5	26

Table 11.1 *The number of different types of courses held, and the number of trainers trained*

> **The sweet smell of success**
>
> Mr Chandradasa and his wife Karuna Hewawdana live in Pallegama, and both attended food processing training courses in 1994. They have now started to make and sell several types of confectionery. Mr Chandradasa used to work as a co-operative manager in town but since starting their own business, he has left that job to devote his time more fully to marketing the *jujubes*, *batto*, *rulang* toffee and milk toffee they make.
>
> Before embarking on this venture, Mr Chandradasa visited several local shop owners and traders and asked if there was a demand for anything which they did not stock. He was able to do this easily as he used to distribute tea and therefore had contact with traders. Initially the couple contacted the Mahaweli Entrepreneur Development Organization (MEDO), who not only funded their attendance on the courses but also provided assistance in supplying the necessary equipment, and working capital in order to begin production. In order to get this assistance and support, the Chandradasas had to convince MEDO of the profitability of the idea (i.e. produce a simple business plan).
>
> The business entails the production of two batches of *jujubes* per week. Each batch takes about five hours to produce from start to finish, but other jobs can be done during the production process, while the product is setting for example. It costs Rs500 for the raw materials and the products are sold for a total of Rs700. They also make 750 pieces of *rulang* toffee a week, sold in packets of 50 pieces; the same amount of milk toffee, and 300 packets of *batto*. Both raw materials and rolls of plastic film for packaging are available in Pallegama – an area of Embilipitiya close to where they live. Labels are produced locally, but they are unhappy with the poor quality as this affects the marketing of their products. They have now increased turnover to such an extent that they can reinvest their savings in a purpose-built workshop for confectionery production. Training has helped them make much more of their lives.

organizations throughout Asia. An international workshop, with an emphasis on Asian regions, was held in Sri Lanka in July 1997.

Programmes for students. Training in small-scale food processing is offered to undergraduates of universities or affiliated colleges, as requested by the respective institutions.

Table 11.1 summarizes the number and type of courses held between 1992 and 1995.

The benefits of training

The training courses focus on the needs of small-scale agricultural producers and food processors making food products for the market, with a view to increasing their productivity and incomes. Agricultural production is seasonal. IT Sri Lanka provides training support to institutions with an emphasis on adding value to agricultural products and to strengthening the capability of small agricultural producers to negotiate in the market.

Women are likely to be more disadvantaged than men in the above groups. One-fifth of the country's households are headed by women, over 70 per cent of whom are widows. Almost half the agricultural labourers are women and one-fifth of the female labour force are deployed as unpaid family workers. It should be noted that the aim of promoting income generation for women is not merely welfare, but to improve women's long-term equality in access to resources and their empowerment.

The training courses have been regularly evaluated to measure their impact and find ways to improve them. The first internal evaluation was carried out in 1991. The second evaluation in 1993 was external, as was the evaluation in 1996/97.

Training of trainers course. The annual Cathy Rich Memorial Training Course has trained more than 60 fieldworkers who have provided training to over 3700 people. As a result, over 250 successful businesses have been established providing employment for more than 1000 people. An example of the impact of this on people's lives is given in the box describing Mr Chandradasa.

Short courses. More than 200 entrepreneurs have received training on the short courses. This has resulted in increased profits for more than 120 of them.

University courses. Over 50 students have been trained on the university courses. Working with universities and academic institutions has provided an opportunity to influence the future decisionmakers to pay adequate attention to small-scale agro-processing. Initially, working with students was difficult, as they expect to learn about new and sophisticated technology. They sometimes feel that to promote the small-scale technologies that are used by rural communities is to take a step backwards, when the current trend is towards greater sophistication. However, once convinced, they can be highly committed to promoting appropriate technologies.

As a result of the training of trainers courses, 228 new food processing enterprises were established and continue to function. In addition, the new enterprises have helped improve around 1000 existing enterprises. The Tamil training of trainers course participants have already identified 216 potential enterprises in the plantation sector.

Short courses are only held on demand. This demand has increased from two per year in 1992/93 to five per year in 1996/97, which indicates the value placed on the courses by the entrepreneurs. Monitoring of the short courses has shown that most trainees take a more positive approach to implementing hygienic practices and improvements to technology.

Lessons learnt

Support and follow-up are essential

Support and follow-up are an important aspect of training. Trainers need support for the first activities they do after acquiring training skills. If they run into problems they get disheartened and demoralized easily and think that they cannot handle the task. IT Sri Lanka trainers visit these trainees to provide the initial support. Trainers can only be successful if they receive sufficient support from their organization and their organizations have realistic targets for them. Fieldworkers usually have little decision-making power within their organization, however, and IT Sri Lanka intervenes to create a better working environment for extension workers by influencing decision-makers within their organization. It is important to ensure that decision-makers understand and support the training work. IT Sri Lanka has developed relationships with them and key vocational, entrepreneurship and leadership development institutions throughout the country.

Not all participants realize the full implications of putting what they will learn into practice. This is covered in detail during the first phase of the training programme and the participants and their organizations can decide whether they want to continue with training. If they decide that the course does not meet their expectations, they do not have to participate in the following two modules of the training of trainers course.

Sharing experiences is beneficial

Trainers are encouraged to meet regularly and help each other to solve problems, based on their own experiences. They act as resource persons to each other. To encourage the sharing of information, IT actively promotes networking among past trainees. Through regular meetings, extension workers share experiences and ideas which motivates them to be innovative and active. IT is planning to develop training facilities in the local areas where previous trainees can pool their resources and conduct training programmes.

Ensuring that training meets the specific needs of women

More than 80 per cent of the trainers are women. This intentional bias is because the majority of small-scale food processors are women and women trainers are more suited to assist village-level women food processors. There are a number of economical, political and social reasons why women find it difficult to establish small businesses or improve their businesses. The constraints faced by women and successful and unsuccessful examples of problem alleviation are discussed on training courses to find better methods of tackling these issues in the field. One of the main constraints is that women often have to rely on a male relative to purchase raw material and to market the product. Although some women eventually become able to work independently, particularly if they are from a female-headed household, support from male relatives is very significant at the beginning, even if it is from a young boy.

Participating in a training programme may be difficult for a woman due to social reasons. For example, if the programme is conducted by a man, if it is held in an inconvenient place, if it is difficult to travel to, or if the timing does not fit in with her other activities. Women may not be able to afford the time to participate in the programmes. Trainers can overcome this by going *to* the women, and training of trainers programmes encourage women extension workers to visit women in the informal sector to increase their skills and access to training.

Ideal course length

Most fieldworkers find food processing a new discipline which involves receiving and sharing many new ideas and information. The training of trainers courses therefore need sufficient time to allow this information to be exchanged. However, a balance has to be struck between sufficient length to cover all the details and what is feasible for the course participants. Initially, the training of trainers course was designed as a 45-day residential programme where the basics of food technology as well as marketing and management are discussed in detail. The feedback from participants stressed that this was too long and it was very difficult for fieldworkers (particularly women) to be away from their homes for this length of time. The sending organizations, too, found this a problem particularly if they were a small development organization, as they could not afford to release staff for long periods. The course was redesigned to include a number of smaller modules, some of which are carried out in the field to allow trainees more flexibility.

Beneficiaries' opinions are vital

Some of the modules involve trainers visiting participants. The trainers have found that meeting the trainees in their own working environment not only helps them understand the participants' strengths and problems, but also gives them better motivation to carry out the work. Their individual problems can be highlighted and the extension worker given assistance to resolve them. Depending on the problem, assistance can be provided with further training on a specific technology, having discussions with the sending organizations to improve the extension plan or discussing the problem with the other extension workers during subsequent training to find out how they have addressed similar situations.

Combining the business and technical aspects

Food processing training programmes conducted by most agencies focus on recipes: a product preparation is demonstrated with the necessary instructions to produce it for commercial purposes. This kind of training is very popular, and has a large participation rate, but experience shows that very few enterprises are developed as a result of this and most people from these courses who try to start food processing businesses quickly abandon them. This type of training does not include information about the other factors that are important to achieve success. Training should include other key factors such as resource identification, marketing, bookkeeping and management. Other information includes how to register a business, and how to deal with banks, raw material suppliers, manufacturers, equipment fabricating workshops and new technologies.

We cannot reach the poorest of the poor

IT Sri Lanka has learnt that working with the very poor is impossible. They have more pressing needs such as working in order to get the next meal: they do not have the

Beneficiaries opinions are vital (IT/Kate Clarke)

starting capital for a small business and they cannot afford to spend time on improving skills. Yet, if the small-scale food processing sector is strengthened this could then assist poorer groups also, as they can be employed in successful enterprises.

Good skills do not come free of charge

A number of development agencies conduct programmes in Sri Lanka which are targeted at the poorest of the poor. These programmes are conducted free of charge for participants, or they actually pay them to participate as these recipients cannot otherwise afford to spend time on training. However, many organizations follow the same rule even for those who are not as poor. IT Sri Lanka training charges a fee from all participants. Initially this was difficult, and IT had to award scholarships. As the reputation of the training programmes built up, however, charging fees became less of a problem. The fees are normally subsidized and the participants, especially if they are entrepreneurs, are able to pay at least part of the cost. Charging a fee is also a very good indicator of the demand for the course, as well as how much the recipients feel that they would benefit from these courses.

Collaboration

Linking up with other organizations that conduct training is also beneficial. IT Sri Lanka has assisted a number of organizations to develop their training programmes with IT trainers participating as resource persons. In addition, IT has also helped other agencies to plan their work strengthening the small food processing sector and assisted in developing a food processing business curriculum for the Vocational Training Authority (VTA) of Sri Lanka. VTA intends to establish regional training centres to increase access to vocational training by the unemployed. CRMFPTU will investigate the possibility of collaboration with VTA to increase the access to training facilities by trainers.

University teachers are well respected by policy- and decision-makers and they are usually very influential. It is possible to influence policymakers by allowing university teachers to conduct reviews of work and evaluations, sit on advisory committees and contribute to technical and development research. The academics who worked with the project have become very enthusiastic promoters of the small-scale food processing sectors.

No formal qualifications are required
The trainees are not required to have any minimum qualifications. This is to allow those who have not been able to complete formal education in schools, but are interested and able to develop their skills and knowledge and could contribute to the development of the small-scale food processing sector.

The demand for training
The CRMFPTU is now a fully autonomous body catering to the needs of the small-scale food processing sector in Sri Lanka, particularly on training, while working in collaboration with other relevant organizations to increase the impact. All programmes conducted at CRMFPTU are in response to demand from potential trainees. Courses are only held if there are sufficient participants to cover the costs. CRMFPTU has a very good reputation within Sri Lanka and presently there are more requests than can be accommodated. Most of the requests come from government departments such as the Industrial Development Board, for training extension workers and to assist with their technical enquiries. There is still a demand for training programmes which are carefully designed to cater to the varied needs of the small-scale food processing sector. The CRMFPTU is capable of responding to this demand with high-quality training programmes suitable for a range of individuals.

Further reading
The following evaluation reports are available from IT Sri Lanka or the IT head office in the UK.

1. 'Gender implications of income generating projects: lessons from a training project on food processing', Ariyabandhu, M.M. (1993), IT Sri Lanka.
2. 'An evaluation of the Cathy Rich Rural Food Processing Training Courses', Curran, T. and Banda, R. (1991), IT.
3. 'Evaluation of the Cathy Rich Food Processing Training Programme', Wijetilleka, S. and Gamage, A. (1993), IT Sri Lanka.

12
Women mean business in Sudan
ABDEL GADIR ELIMAM, SUE AZAM-ALI and MIKE BATTCOCK

Introduction

Covering 2.5 million square kilometres the Sudan is the largest country in Africa. It has a population of 25 million people, of whom 25 per cent live in urban areas and 75 per cent in rural areas. The country is considered to be among the poorest in the world, despite a wealth of human and natural resources. Many traditional rural skills have been retained, particularly among the poorer communities. Sudan has a rich heritage in the field of food processing, with a variety of sophisticated and interesting food products, especially fermented products.

The overall level of poverty in Sudan is high, and it is aggravated by very limited health and education services. Employment opportunities in the formal production and government sectors are very limited, so the most hopeful opportunity for absorbing the growing labour force is in the small-scale productive sector. Food processing is particularly suited to small-scale production and women already play an important role in this sector.

Eastern Sudan is considered one of the poorest parts of the country. This region comprises three states: Red Sea, Kassala and Gedaref. Intermediate Technology (IT Sudan's) programme work is concentrated in the two southern states, Kassala and Gedaref, which cover an area of about 135 000 sq.km. Approximately 2.4 million people from a range of ethnic backgrounds (50 per cent rural, 35 per cent urban and 15 per cent nomads) inhabit this area, which is one of the most densely populated areas in the Sudan. The area has a sizeable underemployed labour force and markets for products within the project area as well as good communications with potential markets elsewhere in the country. On the other hand, it relies quite heavily on goods or materials imported from outside Sudan or from elsewhere in the country. However, there is a ready supply of raw materials which hold potential for a range of processing activities.

IT Sudan started work in Eastern Sudan in 1993, following investigations in four parts of the country – Khartoum, Sennar, Port Sudan and Eastern Sudan – which looked at the potential for expanding the productive sector, and the possibilities for intervention. The investigation also considered opportunities for complementary inputs by local partners and for governmental support. The investigation culminated in a seminar in Khartoum in January 1994, jointly organized with the Small Industries Department, and attended by a range of local development organizations. The investigation identified the eastern region as the most suitable area to initiate programme activities because of its broad span of productive technologies, accessibility to local markets, and the relatively large number of poor people recently migrated into the area. In addition, this region was perceived as a good place to create a visible presence for IT Sudan to demonstrate the effectiveness and impact of its integrated and participative approach.

The need

Small-scale food processors in Sudan, who are often women, are responsible for the majority of food products produced and sold in the country. The large-scale formal food production sector is not well developed and the few imported products are expensive. The bulk of food products, particularly those consumed by poorer people, are from

While skills are well developed in traditional areas, training helps to increase product diversity (IT/Mohammed Majzoub)

the small-scale sector. This has led to a high degree of versatility and innovation. However, small producers are relatively isolated, not only from other producers in Sudan but also from the information and innovation occurring elsewhere in the world. Investigations by IT Sudan have identified the following key constraints which limit marginalized and vulnerable groups' access to income and employment opportunities.

Technical skills. While skills are well developed in specific areas, they are limited to a range of traditional food products. For product quality to be improved or product diversity to be increased, new skills are required including: the selection of raw materials, drying techniques, packaging, quality control and food safety and hygiene. There are some training centres which offer training in basic skills, but this does not cater for an improved product range and hence does not address the needs of the market.

Management skills. Small-scale food processing enterprises require competency in a range of management skills in order to survive and grow. The food processing sector is undergoing considerable changes and in particular, new entrants often lack the necessary business management skills. Weaknesses have been identified as financial management (costing, accounts and credit management), time management, marketing and managing the production process.

The availability of information. There is a shortage of information for planning or taking decisions on new food products or expansion of production e.g. prices, markets, products, processes and equipment. Such information would be useful for development organizations and government departments. When data are available (e.g. from the Department of Statistics and Government Planning Units), it is often not in a form readily usable by such organizations.

Finance. Access to capital is limited for small businesses. Although some banks do provide credit for small business, many do not. Some government agencies (e.g. Takaful) provide support in the form of grants, as do some development organizations (e.g. Human Appeal).

Development of the training programme

In response to specific requests by partner organizations, IT Sudan initiated food processing training activities. The overall objective of the training courses is to improve the livelihoods of poor families in Eastern Sudan through improved incomes, employment and food security. This will be achieved by enabling women to establish successful small businesses making food products and increase the domestic processing of food for improved food security.

Participant selection

The selection of participants for training courses is carried out jointly by IT Sudan and the project partners. A variety of criteria is used:

o participants must be serious about establishing a small business;
o women should be from the poorer families in the village;
o the sending organization should be committed to supporting participants after they receive training; and
o participants need to be able to read and write if they are being trained as trainers.

Women trainees on this course in Sudan benefited from talking to one another and learning from others' experiences (IT/Mohammed/Majzoub)

Course content

Suaad El Bagir Ahmed of the Khartoum Food Research Centre, developed the course after investigating the raw materials available in Eastern Sudan and the market potential of the products made. The first course in January 1994 was to train trainers, in a range of fruit and vegetable drying techniques. The course lasted one month, training 27 female fieldworkers from nine development organizations. These women have then been the trainers for later IT Sudan food processing training courses. The courses cover the following areas:

o introduction to food processing;
o solar dehydration;
o preservation techniques;

> **Ms Sanaa**
>
> Sanaa is 29 years old and has completed high school education. She works as an assistant accountant where she earns Ls 10 000 (US$8) per month. Sanaa is part of a large family of ten of whom five are still at school. Her father is a pensioner with a monthly income of Ls 7000 (US$6) which is inadequate to support his family and Sanaa therefore has to contribute to the household expenses. She was nominated to attend the IT Sudan food processing course. As a result of the training, she has now established her own business making processed fruits, jams, dried meat, onion and granulated fruit juice drinks. Her original profession helped her to plan and identify market needs before production. Sanaa started her business with a loan of Ls 15 000 (US$12.5). She now earns about Ls 25 000 (US$20) each month from the sale of mixed fruit jams and dried fruit juice granules. Her products are of a high quality and she has no problems in marketing them. The majority are sold to colleagues, neighbours and traditional retailers. Sanaa is planning to produce granulated dried fruit juice and dried lentil soup for sale to customers in Kassala during Ramadan. Her ambition is to see her business develop to a larger scale.

- packaging;
- storage;
- hygiene;
- marketing; and
- business development.

Participants are formed into work teams and work together throughout the course. This provides an opportunity for the women to gain skills of working together to produce food products to a deadline, and provides an opportunity to gain experience managing a team of people.

Dried fruits and vegetables have a high market demand and IT Sudan has produced an illustrated booklet in Arabic covering the technical aspects of producing a high-quality packaged dried product. As new product areas have been identified, they have been added to the course, including jams and cheese (see box describing Ms Sanaa's production of such foods). A booklet on the production of jams and juices has been produced. The products being considered for future courses include halva, pastries, juices, toffees and peanut brittle. There has been one special course run by the training manager from Intermediate Technology Bangladesh introducing a range of Bangladeshi food products to the Sudanese trainers.

During follow-up visits, marketing was identified as a key constraint. In response to this, a special refresher course on marketing was held in 1996. This course included pricing the product, promotion, distribution and simple marketing techniques. A marketing game developed by OEF International and included in the book *Marketing Strategy* by Suzanne Kindervatter was used, which was very popular and useful. In this game, participants answer questions on marketing to move around a board. All the players discuss the answers and agree whether the person's answer was sufficient to allow them to move on further. This discussion brings out many issues and allows the participants to share their knowledge and experience.

Follow-up

On most of the courses, two or three fieldworkers from the partner organization are trained alongside the women beneficiaries. These fieldworkers will then be able to provide long-term follow-up for the women.

IT Sudan has worked with the women trained to establish mutual support groups. In Kassala, the Kassala Women's Development Society was established in 1995, the Hawatta Women's Development Society in 1996 and the Gedaref Women's Development Society in 1996. These groups carry out a variety of activities, ranging from accessing raw materials and identifying new products to improving marketing knowledge and skills. The women have carried out a survey of market traders to identify the different food products on sale, packaging materials used and the product quality. These surveys resulted in strong linkages between the society and women market traders.

Monitoring and evaluation

At the end of each course there is a short examination to see how much of the technical information the participants have learnt. There is also a short questionnaire to find out the views of the participants on the course. Both the project partners and IT Sudan will follow this up with evaluations after a year.

Project impact

The training is now well established and respected in the area. To date, ten courses have been held passing on skills to 300 women. The fieldworker participants have trained over 1000 women. The training team have been requested to run a training course in Western Sudan.

The direct beneficiaries of the training courses are marginalized and vulnerable women. Before the course most of the women were aged between 20 and 35, single, and unemployed or earning less than 19 000 Sudanese pounds (Ls) (US$16) per month, which is less than the average civil servant's salary. The number of people that have indirectly benefited from the training is estimated at 100 per course. Indirect beneficiaries include the poor communities in Kassala and Gedaref that benefit from the provision of high-quality, low-cost, safe food products.

After the fifth training course, the project was evaluated to determine its relevance, effectiveness and impact on the lives of the recipients. This was carried out by external independent consultants, the Mustasharat Group. The following is a summary of their findings.

Food security

Over 50 per cent of the women trained now feel that they are food secure. The quality of existing preserved foods had improved and methods of preservation were applied to foods not previously preserved. The training project had a significant impact on preparation, preservation practices and on food expenditure. After the training, women spent less of their income on food because they used more preserved, processed food. The income saved was available for other expenditure (for example, school fees, as in the case of Ms Neimat described in the box). This aspect showed that the women were taking a flexible approach to food processing and were willing to adopt the new ideas.

Incomes and employment

Of the trainees interviewed, 37 per cent had increased their incomes as a result of the training course. Increases in employment were seen in a number of ways: through the creation of new opportunities, self-employment and part-time employment. Those that were not successful at improving their employment opportunities were hampered by financial, marketing and industrial constraints.

One of the main aims of the training course is to create economic independence. To achieve this, it is essential that the women are linked to micro-lending institutions which have a genuine interest in small-scale businesses. The majority of women interviewed in the evaluation had not noticed a significant increase in income following the training

---

Ms Neimat Zein Elabdeen

Neimat is a housewife and mother of five children. Her husband is an agricultural worker earning Ls 10 000 (US$8) per month, which is insufficient to support his family. Neimat tried tailoring to supplement the family income, but faced several difficulties. She attended the IT Sudan food processing training course which has helped to make her life a little easier. Neimat buys fruit and vegetables when they are readily available and cheap, dries them and then sells them for a higher price when availability is low. She usually produces dried onion, tomato and fruit juice granules. At the moment, Neimat is not keeping accounts and cannot determine the exact income generated from this work. However, the income she gains is used for basic family needs and to send the children to school. The impact the project has had can be summed up in her own words: 'Thanks to God and to the IT administration who make my life tolerable'.

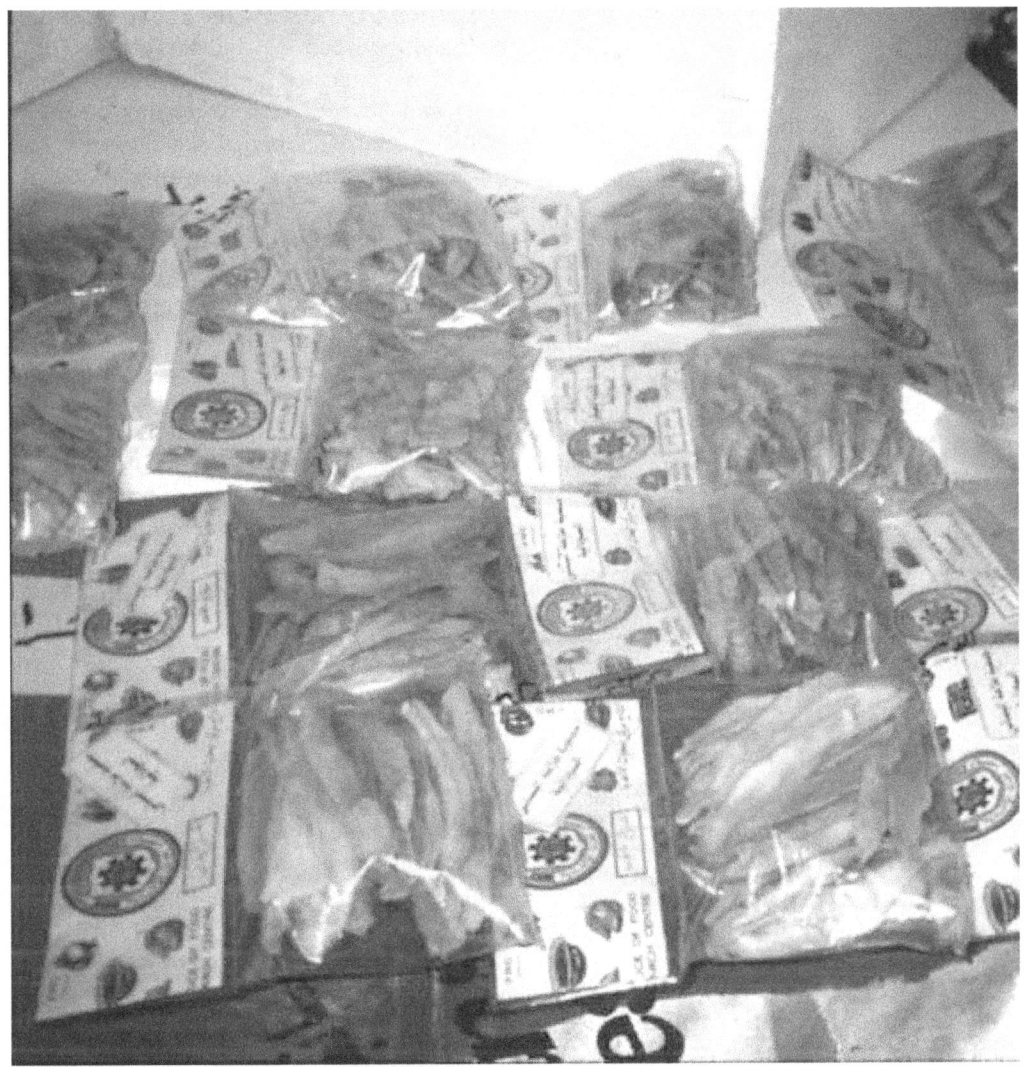

Trainees often need guidance in the areas of packaging, marketing and business skills in addition to product development (IT/Mohammed Majzoub)

course. However, there were notable exceptions. Members of the Takaful organization who had the back-up of credit to assist with implementation of the training witnessed increased incomes. Prior to the training, nine out of ten trainees had no source of income. However, after training, the number of those without an income was halved and the remainder earned between Ls 10 000 and 19 000 (US$8–16) per month. Income was generally spent on basic needs such as food, education and health. There is no indication of whether these priorities changed as a result of the training. As the project is still in its infancy, there is still tremendous scope for improvement.

An indirect benefit of the training courses was the institutional strengthening of local organizations. For example, both Takaful Fund and Human Appeal International have included development issues in their strategies in addition to the provision of financial aid. The training syllabus was included in the curriculum of the Department of Nutrition and School Gardening.

Lessons learnt

Follow up and support in the field. The trainers trained need technical follow-up visits to help overcome problems they face. Trainers who work for well-organized and resourced organizations are more likely to receive this sort of support. The ability of an organization to offer follow-up support should be a criterion for the selection of participants.

The mutual support provided by the Women's Development Societies has proved a very successful way of providing support in the field. These umbrella organizations take the responsibility for organizing credit and savings schemes, providing production information and marketing back-up and organizing training and development programmes.

Participation in the development of the course. The participants need to be involved in the development of the course design and schedule. This ensures that the courses directly meet the needs of the people they are intended for. Because trainers and trainees will have different needs, it is advisable to devise two types of training rather than trying to combine the two.

Balance of technical and business aspects. There needs to be a balance between subjects. Technical process-orientated as well as business-orientated subjects are all essential components of a successful small enterprise. Where appropriate, the business sessions should be related to a food product and complemented by a practical session. In all the modules, a mixture of practical and theoretical sessions will greatly improve the acceptability of the course.

Organization. There need to be sufficient raw materials and equipment for the practical sessions. Good organization before the course is essential.

Clear goals. It is important to formulate the objectives of the course with easily identifiable goals and indicators.

The trainers. Ideally, the trainers should be aged between 20 and 45 years. They should be educated at least to secondary level and be dedicated to passing on their skills to others. Plenty of spare time is required, so training and follow-up can be carried out effectively. Trainers should preferably be trained in nutrition education, extension work or social advice and should be given extensive training on methods of food preservation, so they are in a position to advise.

The beneficiaries. Most of the beneficiaries are aged between 15 and 55 years and preferably from a female-headed household. It is essential that they have back-up support (e.g. production, marketing) and spending power to purchase raw materials either through access to credit or from their own savings.

Conclusion

The approach to training should be a holistic one. Training cannot exist on its own – it should be one element of a larger package. This consists of a number of factors relevant to the development of small businesses, including access to credit, consistent supply of raw materials and equipment, access to a suitable place for production, and the existence of a buoyant market for the products.

Further reading

The following evaluation reports are available from IT Sudan and the IT head office in the UK.

1. 'Training of trainers' course in food processing', Abdel Gadir Elimam (1997), IT Sudan.
2. 'Assessment of the ITDG agro-processing project', Mustasharat Group (1996).

13
Food processing training in Uganda
BARRIE AXTELL, PETER FELLOWS and MIKE DILLON

Introduction and background

Uganda, in central east Africa, is a country rich in natural resources and, due to its altitude, blessed with a sub-tropical climate. A wide range of tropical and sub-tropical crops are grown, including fruits, such as banana and pineapple, coffee and tea. Lake Victoria is an important source of fish, much of which is now exported to Europe. The country has a strong tradition of dairy production, and milk and milk products have a good market.

Uganda had the misfortune to suffer 25 years of social and political instability under a series of regimes. It has recently returned to a state of political and social stability, but the impact of those 25 years is still apparent. It is, however, now an environment open to economic development particularly in the manufacturing sector which is seeing substantial growth.

In 1994 Midway Technology Ltd, a UK company dedicated to providing assistance to small- and medium-scale enterprises, joined in partnership with the Uganda Manufacturers' Association (UMA) to design and deliver a training programme to strengthen the food processing sector. UMA is the largest organization in Uganda repres-

Drying is a popular course subject (Midway Technology)

enting the interests of the private sector, in particular the manufacturing sector. It is a highly respected organization with over 500 members including large, medium and small enterprises, banks and forwarding agencies.

UMA's objectives are:

o to promote, protect and co-ordinate the interests of industrialists in Uganda;
o to act as a watchdog and an effective mouthpiece for its members;
o to initiate and facilitate discussions and information exchange between members; and
o to advise government on key policies affecting industry.

In its large show-ground at Lugogo near Kampala UMA facilities include an industrial and trade information centre, an economic desk and a newly opened training centre. In addition the show-ground hosts frequent international trade fairs. UMA is thus a partner of strength with a solid track record of fostering industrial development.

The first training programme

At the outset UMA and Midway clearly defined the target beneficiaries of training as owners and operatives of existing small and medium enterprises and others with a serious interest in establishing food processing units. It was agreed that the target group would not include either microenterprises, as the course materials were not appropriate to their circumstances, or large-scale enterprises, which could afford independent consultants.

The UMA–Midway partnership resulted in the submission of a proposal for a six-week course entitled 'Food processing as an industrial enterprise', that received funding from the British Council under its In-Country Training Programme in 1994.

The course was over-subscribed three fold, and was attended by 60 participants, mainly drawn from existing food processing enterprises. The enterprises typically had 5 to 20 staff, one exception being a larger bakery with over 100 on the payroll. All of the participants attended the initial week of the course, during which the basic principles of food spoilage and preservation together with aspects related to marketing, costing, quality control, packaging and financial management were covered. During the subsequent weeks participants, in groups of no more than 20, carried out practical production of dairy, bakery, honey, fruit and vegetable products. A final week of training was provided for all participants, during which they were assisted in the development of a business plan for their own enterprise that could be submitted to a financial institution.

A post-course evaluation indicated that the participants had received considerable benefit from their training and led UMA and Midway to prepare a project proposal for a five-year programme of assistance to the food processing sector. A central objective of this project was to identify and train a cadre of Ugandan trainers so that UMA would have a locally sustainable resource to assist its members. This project was approved by the British Overseas Development Administration, (now the Department for International Development) and began in 1995. As the project moved into its third year in 1997 the emphasis increasingly moved to training of trainers courses, with Ugandan trainers increasingly being involved in the design, preparation and delivery of courses. In addition, some of these trainers have been trained and are undertaking specific work for enterprises on a consultancy basis. To date, over 300 people have attended the courses, some of them returning several times.

Both UMA and Midway now consider that the basic methodology developed for the food processing sector is applicable to other sectors, such as engineering, carpentry, silk and textiles. In order to deliver such a wide range of courses, it is recognized that an efficient training centre needs to be established with staff trained to operate all the required administrative systems to meet the needs of Ugandan enterprises. These needs, which have been expressed by manufacturers and identified through formal surveys and informal feedback, include the

> **Session title: Food spoilage for engineers**
>
> *Objectives*
> At the end of the session participants will be able to:
>
> 1. Describe the factors that cause food spoilage.
> 2. Describe the most important factors related to engineering design (microbiological spoilage and contamination with soils).
> 3. Know that micro-organisms can be classified into bacteria, moulds and yeasts.
> 4. Know their requirements for growth.
> 5. Describe how and where micro-organisms can grow in equipment.
> 6. Describe how other sources of contamination (through the reaction of food with construction materials, foreign bodies) are related to equipment design.
>
> NB: participants will be unfamiliar with this area and simple language should be used and names of specific organisms avoided where possible.
>
> *Time allowed: 2 hrs*
> *Materials required: flipchart, pens, handout Nos 1–6, mouldy bread or cheese, if available mouldy peanuts.*
>
> *Notes*
> 1. Trainer explains micro-organisms are everywhere. Few are harmful, most beneficial. Life would not exist without them. Open discussion of examples of micro-organisms that participants know about.
> 2. Micro-organisms of importance in foods are mould, yeast and bacteria. Explain the characteristics of each and that they can be divided into spoilage, useful and harmful organisms.
> 3. Use brainstorm to develop a list under these three headings on flipchart.
> 4. Trainer uses buzz to extract 'requirements for growth'. Introduce aerobic and anaerobics.
> 5. Introduce term pathogens, cover the most important ones.

Figure 13.1 *Part of the trainer lesson plan*

provision of information, books, ingredients, packaging and equipment that are not available in Uganda, and individual consultancy to deal with individuals' specific problems. At the time of writing UMA has formally taken the decision to establish a training centre, a manager has been recruited and Midway is reducing its responsibility for arranging and managing UMA courses.

Midway has established a not-for-profit support centre with Ugandan directors. The centre acts as a 'one-stop shop' for entrepreneurs and trainers who wish to have training and consultancy services or purchase books, materials and equipment. The centre intends to be financially self-sustaining within the next two years. Midway is supporting the centre with training of trainers and consultants courses and the provision of technical inputs.

The approach to training

The training courses follow a clearly agreed format that comprises:

- *Design* of courses based on participants' needs, as identified and agreed through surveys, interviews and feedback and formal evaluations.
- *Delivery* using highly participative techniques and learning by doing.
- *Discussion and evaluation* with participants to ensure the relevance of what has been learnt to their own businesses.
- *Impact* through post-course evaluations and follow-up.

Midway's first requirement when providing training was to be sure that the courses offered met the perceived needs of the participants. Midway and UMA met with owners and managers of food processing enterprises to discuss their needs, and objectives were agreed for all the programmes. In the Ugandan context it was clear that broad enterprise development support was required covering all aspects of business management and including technical training. The overall objective was to provide business and technical support to the sector by assisting

> **Food processing as an industrial enterprise**
>
> *Foreign bodies*
> Foreign bodies are for most companies the major source of customer complaints. Foreign bodies can get into foods in many ways, including poor design of equipment. A major British food company analysed its foreign body complaints a few years ago. It found that of the 13 477 complaints received, 6289 or 47 per cent could have been partly or totally due to defects in machinery or its design.
>
> | Complaint type | Number | % of total |
> | --- | --- | --- |
> | Dirt | 1303 | 9.7 |
> | Metal, ferrous | 966 | 7.2 |
> | Plastic and rubber | 963 | 7.1 |
> | Oil and grease | 762 | 5.6 |
> | String | 587 | 4.4 |
> | Wood | 571 | 4.2 |
> | Fibres | 525 | 3.9 |
> | Glass | 257 | 1.9 |
> | Bristles | 202 | 1.5 |
> | Metal, non-ferrous | 153 | 1.1 |
>
> In addition there were 1166 insect complaints, a proportion of which could be attributed to poor equipment design.
> If this data had been taken 20 years earlier it is certain that wood and paint chip complaints would have been high. Now the use of wood and painted surfaces has been replaced by stainless steel.
>
> **Be aware of foreign body risks when designing equipment**
> Midway Technology and Uganda Manufacturers' Association

Figure 13.2 *A typical handout used in Ugandan Courses.*

entrepreneurs to develop existing or potential new businesses. The programme would help industries, sometimes in specifically targeted subsectors, such as bakery or dairy, to develop a better understanding of the business aspects of their enterprise and the environment in which they had to compete. Other courses such as marketing, product development and quality assurance were designed to be suitable for all subsectors.

Design, planning and preparation

A series of lesson plans were prepared for each module, including the practical production sessions, which included trainers' guides, overheads and handouts. Handouts are considered an important component of the courses as they provide participants with a written summary of all areas covered for future reference. One page of a typical lesson plan is shown in Figure 13.1, while an associated handout is shown in Figure 13.2.

The example in Figure 13.1 shows how the simple 'Plan objectives, delivery methods, required support materials and activities system' is used for each session within a training module. The activities are expanded upon by the trainer, the delivery style being related to the session objectives and group needs. One trainer may, for example, achieve understanding through group discussion while another may select role play.

Facilities

The delivery of theoretical sessions has caused few problems as suitable training rooms are available at UMA or in other institutions. The practical sessions have, however, caused considerable difficulties. No suitable facility exists within UMA and trainers have been forced to use other institutions, for example the home economics room of a school and the canteen of a large institute. These facilities have been far from ideal in terms of hygiene, security, water and power supplies. No dedicated practical training facility exists in Uganda, with the exception of the Dairy Corporation's training unit at Entebbe and mechanical engineering workshops. The lack of a dedicated site caused much frustration among trainers and participants, with meals having to be delivered by car, the lack of a place to eat lunch, all equipment needing to be packed away in a safe store each night with resultant loss of class time, and difficult working conditions in mechanical engineering workshops. Despite all these problems, practical session evaluations by participants were very positive. Indeed a bond grew between the participants and their trainers as everybody had to pull together and face each day's frustration.

A wide range of 'Food Processing as an Industrial Enterprise' courses have been held from 1994 and these are summarized in Figure 13.3.

Course title

o Basic bakery skills
o Honey processing
o Fruit and vegetable processing
o Dairy products
o Design of food processing equipment
o Advanced bakery skills
o Quality management and assurance
o Edible oil extraction
o Developing and marketing new products
o Training of trainers
o Training of technical advisers

These last two courses are designed to teach local trainers or advisers how to plan, develop and deliver courses and assist local enterprises in an advisory capacity

---

Figure 13.3 *The range of courses held by Midway Technology in association with UMA*

A central objective of the training programme is to establish a financially self-sustaining unit by the end of the project. Clearly one key element is a team of skilled Ugandan trainers able to develop and deliver required courses. In Uganda, as in most countries, much 'training' is little more than lecturing. In many cases participative methods are unfamiliar, indeed many highly skilled staff from universities and institutions find such methods disturbing and even threatening. Superficially, participative methodology removes much control from the trainer. The participants gain confidence, may often question the trainer aggressively, and can appear to take control. The truth is that a well-prepared participative trainer is always in control, has set aims and objectives and has the flexibility to change pace or cover the often unplanned interests of the participants. The approach results in training that is geared to the specific and individual needs of participants. It encourages involvement and the sharing of experiences and has been shown, by evaluations, to be a very effective way of learning.

Training of trainers and advisers

By the end of 1997, three Training of Trainers (TOT) courses had been held for individuals who had shown potential training skills and aptitudes. Many of these were drawn from among participants who attended previous courses. The courses cover the identification of training needs, selection of participants, course planning (session times, content, methods), the use of audio-visual materials, teaching practical skills, use of participative techniques and monitoring sessions through feedback. All TOT participants prepare and deliver individual sessions during the two-week course and they are given individual feedback from both the trainer and from other participants.

There is also an identified need for advisers who are able to visit individual enterprises to offer specialist assistance in both business and technical areas. It was considered that these advisers or consultants, who would provide services on a fee-paying basis, would require training to upgrade their skills. By 1997, a two-week course had been delivered for advisers. It covered areas including contracts and agreements, costing work, budgets, confidentiality, customer

> **Week 1**
> Day 1. Introduction, basic food composition, spoilage and preservation. Formation of participants into groups.
> Day 2. Selling and marketing. Identification of market segments, consumer surveys, calculation of market size and value, used to calculate scale of production. Includes short market surveys in local retail outlets.
> Day 3. Calculation of scale of production. Groups work on their selected products. Methods of selling, advertising, samples, company image, label design and the law.
> Day 4. Stages in processing. Application of quality assurance procedures, cost calculations, yields and record keeping to each stage of the process, using identified foods for each group.
> Day 5. Calculating profitability. Fixed and variable costs, depreciation, calculation of income and gross profit, the need for feasibility studies, why do them, what they should contain, getting information, planning work for future weeks.
>
> **Week 2**
> Practical production sessions working in teams and incorporating all business and quality aspects covered in week 1.
>
> **Week 3**
> Teams develop their own production ideas.
>
> **Week 4**
> Participants return to develop business feasibility study.

Figure 13.4   *Course structure*

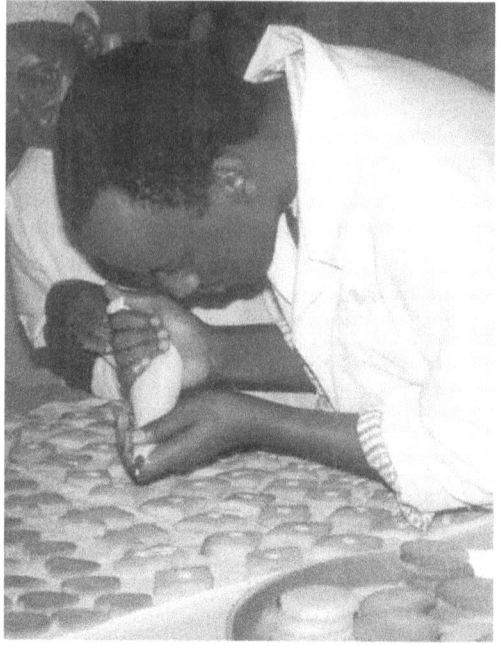

A training course is offered to bakers and confectioners (Midway Techology)

relations and reporting. This aspect of the programme is expected to become more important in the next phase of the project.

The first course to be designed and delivered by local trainers was held in a local dairy in early 1997 and at the time of writing two further local courses are planned. Current indications are that these local courses will break even if 12 participants attend.

Course structure and content

While the particular contents of specific sub-sector modules, such as bakery or drying, will clearly vary, all courses follow a similar basic format. During the first week basic theory, both technical and business, is presented as shown in Figure 13.4.

The overall style of training is highly participative. The training room layout avoids the traditional rows of forward-facing desks and established participative techniques, such as brainstorming, buzz groups and hum groups are used. Key pages from flipcharts are hung around the room for future reference and as a reminder. Participants are encouraged to voice information, experiences, skills and problems they have encountered in their own business to be shared by all. All trainers have been formally prepared in participative techniques and traditional lecturing is discouraged. During the second week the groups (which by now have established a company name, logo and label) produce a range of food items, such as bakery goods, dairy products or dried foods, depending on the specific course.

These manufacturing sessions are designed to develop and apply both technical and business skills. Each day managers are selected to be responsible for the teams' production. The course tutors place orders for specific foods, with the manager stating their delivery requirements, such as net weight of packs, appearance and sugar levels. Managers then plan the production with their team. Any equipment required has to be 'hired' from the tutor and its cost calculated in terms of depreciation. The products are then manufactured, packaged, costed and inspected to determine if they are of a marketable quality and standard. Both technical and management skills are observed by the tutors and at the end of the day an open discussion is held. During this the tutors can point to errors or improvements that could be made in production, management style and performance to achieve more efficient production. The managers analyse their role and the team 'workers' comment on the managers' methods. It is found that by the end of five days most participants are able to undertake product costings, plan production, control hygiene and implement quality control.

During the third week, individual participants are encouraged to develop products in which they have a particular interest. In general it is found that several small groups with a similar product idea bond together. At the end of the week a review examines all the information that needs to be brought together in order to prepare a feasibility study for the selected products. Finally, after a space of about a month to allow for further market testing and information gathering, participants are invited to a final week's tuition during which they are assisted in the preparation of a feasibility study and business plan that could be submitted to funders.

The same general approach is used on a new course entitled 'The design and manufacture of food processing equipment'. This course differs in that it is targeted at engineers and owners of small workshops which have the capacity to build equipment for food processing enterprises. In line with the normal format, the first week is devoted to theory: the design process, teamworking, planning, materials specifications and the basics of food composition, micro-biology, and public health risks that need to be considered in designing hygienic, safe machines. During the second and third weeks the engineers, working in teams, design and construct a selected item of equipment. To date these have included an impulse heat sealer, bottle capping machines, a tray drier, a 10kW bakery oven and a yoghurt pot sealer. At the end of the course the participants know how to cost their equipment and find markets for it among small and medium food processors.

Evaluation

Ongoing monitoring by participants of each day's training is important. A session evaluation form is completed by each participant for each component of the course. These forms, combined with regular discussions with the groups, enable the trainer to measure whether learning is occurring and to modify or re-inforce problem areas as he or she goes along.

The post-course evaluation of the 1994 programme showed that both turnover and profits had increased in some of the businesses surveyed, that 18 full-time jobs had been created directly as a result of the training, that in several enterprises quality assurance and hygiene programmes had been introduced and that new products had been introduced to the market. Two years later a further three companies had been started as a result of the courses. The manager of the large bakery that sent several participants stated that it was 'the most concise, accurate and behaviour-changing programme my staff have been on in the last ten years'. The box on the following page summarizes some of the evaluation's findings.

Two problems were identified: insufficient time for individual product development and the need for more business training. This feedback was used to modify later courses and new courses have been developed specifically to target areas such as market research, new product development and marketing.

> **Some impacts of training in Uganda**
>
> *Bakery*
> One participant promoted to manager of a newly opened bakery with creation of six new jobs. Hygiene and quality programmes introduced, four new products (biscuits, fruit bread, mixed grain bread and pizza) introduced.
>
> *Dairy 1*
> Profits up 20 per cent after implementing quality systems, new fruit puree dairy food introduced.
>
> *Dairy 2*
> New products developed, market research methods now used, quality and hygiene systems introduced.
>
> *Fruit processors*
> Output doubled to 400 jars of jam per week.
>
> *Honey processors*
> Started to pack and market honey.
>
> *General*
> Hygiene improved, staff changing facilities and uniforms introduced.

Advantages and disadvantages of the training approach

On the positive side, the UMA–Midway approach has been shown to be:

- responsive to the actual needs of food processors;
- able to provide highly practical training by integrating technical and business aspects of food processing;
- relevant to the scale of small and medium enterprises; and
- capable of developing self-confidence among participants.

Limitations include:

- practical training is more expensive and difficult to manage than theoretical courses;
- the lack of suitable facilities for practical work;
- problems with identifying small companies, especially in rural areas; and
- difficulties in identifying and obtaining packaging, ingredients and appropriate equipment.

UNIDO training programme for women entrepreneurs in the food processing industry – experiences from Tanzania and Thailand

GABRIELE HERRMANN and TEZER ULUSAY DE GROOT

Background

Food processing is an activity that is most suitable for women both because it is an extension of their farming activities and it offers business opportunities at a small-scale production level with limited capital and facilities. However, such opportunities should be exploited to the full with a forward-looking strategy, and not remain as temporary income generation measures. It is possible to turn food processing into an industrial activity for women, albeit at the micro or small scale. Significant successes have been observed among women who have been able to produce nutritious food hygienically and to sell it both in local and export markets, given the right type of stimulation and assistance.

The UNIDO training programme was developed following a workshop organized with INSTRAW (UN International Research and Training Institute for the Advancement of Women) in 1984, where the rationale for a training programme targeting women was determined. In 1985, draft training modules were developed covering issues such as general management, training of trainers, project promotion services, entrepreneurship and finance. A training needs assessment in four SADCC (Southern African Development Co-ordination Conference) countries (Botswana, Malawi, Zambia and Zimbabwe) was conducted to identify training needs. A workshop in curriculum development with the Pan African Institute for Development–East and Southern Africa (PAID-ESA) as a counterpart was attended by business women and trainers.

Participants were able to learn how to make soy sauce (G. Herrmann)

It was also recognized that technology training was needed for a profit-making business. After consultation with UNIFEM (UN Development Fund for Women), food processing was chosen as the most appropriate area, because of the crucial role played by women in the food cycle. As an extension of their work at home, food processing is a popular and promising subsector for women in small-scale businesses and microenterprises. In some parts of Africa, up to 80 per cent of food is processed by women.

After analysing several training approaches, UNIDO developed curricula and training materials. The entrepreneurship and management materials were developed by the Cranfield School of Management with inputs from PAID-ESA, while the food processing technology manuals were developed by IT (Intermediate Technology Development Group) of the UK.

The materials were field tested three times in Zambia and Zimbabwe. After each field test a number of modifications was made which resulted in the present training programme. The programme can be used in any country where food processing plays a crucial role. However, adaptation of the training package is required to reflect the specific national business environment, national food consumption patterns and the availability of raw materials and processing equipment. The programme is translated into English, French, Spanish, Kiswahili, Vietnamese and Thai.

The training modules

The objective of the training programme is to provide individual women entrepreneurs with the necessary entrepreneurial and management skills and technological knowledge required to operate a viable small-scale food processing enterprise.

The training programme is written in three volumes: one on entrepreneurship development and business management, one on food technology and a workbook. The contents are as follows:

Volume I (entrepreneurship development and management manual)
○ Recruitment and selection of participants
○ Context of the training course and follow-up activities
○ Evaluation
○ Trainer's guide through the manual
○ Course sessions
  (1) Introduction and entrepreneurial awareness
  (2) Technology choice
  (3) Management skills
  (4) Field study
  (5) Technology skills (including hygiene and packaging)
  (6) Business plan preparation and presentation

Volume II (food technology manual)
Dried food
Vegetable oil extraction
Fruit and vegetable products
Cereal products
Products from pulses
Products from root crops
Nut products
Meat products
Fish products
Dairy products
Beverages

According to local needs, other teaching modules are being included in the programme on waste management, efficient energy use and cleaner production technology.

Needs assessment

A comprehensive needs assessment is conducted in a prospective country to adapt the modules to the local context. The aim is to meet the specific training needs while taking into consideration the institutional capacity, market potentials, raw materials and local eating habits. The needs assessment covers aspects such as the selection of a suitable counterpart training institution, assessment of existing credit facilities, training needs analysis of women entrepreneurs, assessment of the food processing sector, market study for potential food products, the availability of equipment, as well as recommendations for the adaptation of the training manuals. The contents, the curriculum and the training level of the programme may, therefore, be different in each country. Also, the range of food products selected for a specific country does not necessarily correspond to those listed in the manual.

For instance, in the Gambia, it was necessary to add a module on literacy and numeracy for the majority of the trainees. In Malaysia, the manual was shortened to include only training of trainers. Here, the idea was to strengthen the capacity of a local training institute to address food processing and to improve their business management training courses.

In Vietnam, an in-depth analysis was undertaken following the logical framework methodology. The programme is a pilot project for the adaptation of the training material to the Asian context and the manuals have been revised thoroughly and the volume on business management has been updated. The sessions guides were also revised in such a way that by providing examples at two different levels, the programme can address two different target groups (i.e. micro-level and small-scale), depending on the group of trainees. The technology part was also revised, keeping the format and methodology of the African version.

In Tanzania, during the first phase of the project, a need was identified to add a unit on aromatic plants and spices. It was seen that this would provide women entrepreneurs with more opportunities for product diversity and export, by adding value to the locally available raw materials.

The training approach and experiences in replication

The needs assessment, which guides the adaptation of UNIDO's generic five-week training programme to the local context, is considered to be of utmost importance. The approach and the training materials are revised according to the findings of this exercise and the duration is adapted to the requirements of women in each country (for instance, the training in Vietnam is a six-week course).

Before training courses are held, a training of trainers (TOT) course of four weeks is conducted involving trainers from the counterpart institution and other relevant institutions. The trainers are taught training techniques as well as the use of the training manuals by consultant TOT specialists. At the beginning of each training course, participants familiar with more formal teaching tried to object to participative methods and the trainers went back to traditional lecturing. After a short time, however, the participants themselves demanded to continue with participatory training methods and eventually this became a very successful component of the training. For instance, at the end of the TOT workshop, the two most introverted women among the participants demonstrated excellent teaching capabilities. Participative methods not only helped them to gain self-confidence, but also turned them into good trainers.

The training programme follows an action-oriented approach (i.e. 'learning by doing') which emphasizes the active participation of the trainees and the role of the trainer as a facilitator rather than a teacher. Participative training methods such as group work, games and role plays are used to elucidate aspects of personal behaviour and management techniques. All programmes involve practical food production by small groups. Since the vast majority of women operating on a micro-scale have received little or no formal education, the courses are prepared in a simple way using drawings and case studies. Demonstrations, learning from case studies, carrying out participants' own market research and practical exercises are the essence of the training approach. The participants already operating businesses are seen as a source of existing knowledge for others to share. Discussions and counselling of the individuals are important features of the training.

Part of the purpose of training is also to link women entrepreneurs to credit institutions. To facilitate this, women are helped to develop a business plan which is presented to a representative of a bank or other credit institution at the end of the course. Networking with existing support institutions in the business environment for marketing, technology, information and other relevant services is considered to be important for the development of entrepreneurship.

In Vietnam, the project is working in close collaboration with three organizations: the Vietnam Women's Union (which has a credit line for women); the Food Industry Research Institute that carries out research on technologies applicable to medium and large-scale enterprises; HAFREC, an enterprise that researches a limited range of food products that they produce. The project has established a contingency to train the beneficiaries of a UNICEF credit facility in food processing technology and business management principles.

Implementation of the training programme

The training modules are offered to national training institutions or small industry development organizations so that they will be in a position to run the courses with no outside assistance once the UNIDO programme has ended. Once a suitable counterpart organization has been selected, the following sequence of activities takes place:

- The adaptation and development of new training materials (including translation).
- A training of trainers (TOT) course.
- Training courses for 16–20 women entrepreneurs at a time.
- If necessary, equipment for training purposes is obtained for the partner institution.

The technical assistance also includes a follow-up scheme for the entrepreneurs, refresher courses for the trainers, an evaluation of the results and the impact of training.

The UNIDO training programme is being implemented in Africa (Botswana and Tanzania), Asia (Thailand and Vietnam) and Central America (nine participating countries), funded by international donors. In Tanzania the training programme is most advanced, whereas in the other countries the programmes are still under implementation and a full impact evaluation has not yet been conducted.

Modifications from Vietnam and Tanzania

In Vietnam, three changes have been introduced into the training modules:

- The participatory training method used by UNIFEM appears in trainers' guides as part of the manual.
- The business management component is integrated into the technology part. Therefore, there is one volume, not two, as in the other cases for Africa and Central America. It was decided that this would be better, particularly for a woman who is running a very small business and who is both the producer and the manager of her enterprise. She would see the two aspects integrated in a logical flow. It was believed that this would also help the entrepreneur to develop a mentality that would allow her to think of her business in its totality.
- The business management volume has been revised and updated with new management concepts. In addition, the trainers' session guides have been revised with examples addressing two different levels of participants (microenterprises and small-scale producers, depending on the group that is being trained). This provides flexibility to the trainer to adapt his or her course to the level of participants.

The Tanzania project is going through a kind of metamorphosis in its second phase. On the basis of the experience gained in the first phase and the findings of an evaluation, several changes have been introduced in the second phase:

- A new module is being prepared on aromatic plants and spices.
- A formal, rather than *ad hoc*, mechanism of follow-up and monitoring trainees is being introduced with the aim of ensuring the sustainability of the skills and techniques imparted to women entrepreneurs.
- Emphasis is placed on quality assurance. This will involve policy advice to the government as well as the development of standards for the entrepreneurs trained by the project.
- A series of short courses are being organized by the project trainers in order to address specific needs of women entrepreneurs at a given time. During the last two years, about 300 businesswomen have been trained in such programmes.

Lessons learnt

One of the most important preconditions for the success of this training programme is the suitability of the counterpart institution. A comprehensive assessment should be carried out including their policies concerning the subsector and gender, as well as their human resource capacity and personnel policies.

The question of sustainability constitutes a major concern in any training programme. Even when participants pay attendance fees, it is almost impossible to run a financially self-sustaining training programme for poor clients, especially women involved in microenterprise or small-scale production. Therefore, it would be unrealistic to expect a two to three year project to establish such training programmes on a sustainable basis.

It is also possible to look at the issue of sustainability from the point of view of:

- the commitment of the counterpart and its strong ownership of the project;
- the capacity of the counterpart to run the training programme even though external support is required for a longer period;
- the impact of the programme on the target beneficiaries. Improved businesses, increased incomes, better product quality or hygiene, and employment generation are all important aspects of long-term sustainability; and
- Good trainers are often difficult to keep at counterpart institutions since government institutions, which are usually selected as counterparts, often pay much less than the private sector. Trainers need to be committed to stay.

In 1995, UNIDO started to follow a more holistic approach concerning entrepreneurship development for women which is reflected in the 'High Impact Programme for Women Entrepreneurship Development'. This approach covers different aspects of sustainable entrepreneurship development for women and addresses women operating in other entrepreneurial activities, not only food processing. The approach also covers other aspects of enterprise development, such as government training programmes, and access to information, equipment, infrastructure and credit.

Future plans

It is the intention of UNIDO to pursue this programme in two ways. Firstly, new training programmes should be developed and implemented taking into consideration the experience gained and lessons learnt elsewhere.

Secondly, the training programme should be run as part of a new service package that was developed as part of UNIDO's reform process. This programme's objective is to improve women entrepreneurs' competitiveness by developing entrepreneurship. It puts emphasis on developing an enabling environment, addressing the factors (such as the policy and legal framework, raw materials, training, information, technology and financial resources) that create this environment. The High Impact Programmes with a focus on agro-processing will be using the training programme's modules as part of its training and technology components.

Women food processing entrepreneurs in Tanzania

The traditional methods of preservation and food processing in Tanzania are drying, fermentation, germination, milling or pounding, smoking and pickling. These methods are widely practised, but production has been too limited to allow the country to expand its market and production is often of a poor quality. The main reasons for this situation are:

o the lack of a comprehensive marketing strategy, including product development and marketing techniques;
o poor quality assurance and low product-quality standards for local products;
o limited access to improved and cleaner production technologies; and
o a lack of managerial skills.

The UNIDO programme, financially supported by the Austrian Government, is focused on training and supporting women entrepreneurs to increase their resourcefulness, self-confidence, competitiveness and innovative thinking. The training is bringing about a number of changes, such as a greater number of women owning well-established food production enterprises, along with high quality standards, adherence to food safety regulations and certification of products, improved marketing and product development and the use of cleaner production technologies.

Looking beyond training activities, the aim is to enhance the business experience of women entrepreneurs, enabling them to improve their competitiveness and productivity to further expand their businesses, to develop and process new products, such as spices, aromas and essential oils, and to improve their technical know-how relevant to their production process.

The first phase of this project, which started in January 1993, created employment by imparting entrepreneurial skills to over 100 businesswomen engaged in food processing. As of July 1996, seven more courses had been held to improve women's capabilities and chances for gainful employment and higher incomes.

By the end of the second phase, which is scheduled to be completed by November 1998, it is expected that more than 300 women entrepreneurs will have received training to upgrade the technical and managerial aspects of their food processing enterprises. Expectations are that at least 10–15 per cent of the business ventures will be able to grow, creating additional jobs for other business partners or employees.

The availability of locally processed, good-quality food products (more than 15 different products, including cooking oil from sunflower seeds, banana wine, tomato jam, various fruit jams and sweet potato leaves) at competitive prices improves living standards, and, by adding value to local raw materials, contributes to the overall economic development of the country. Approximately 80 per cent of the trained women are in business with assets in equipment and production facilities ranging from US$400 to US$2000.

In the second phase of the project, training is being provided in the use of cleaner production technology, waste management and more efficient energy use.

The women entrepreneurs are organized nationally (Tanzania Food Producers Association) and in regional business associations in order to consolidate training and business services. An important feature of this project is to engage those associations in product development, training and consultancy and advisory services using the 20 trainers trained over two years by the UNIDO programme. Since the associations will be involved in the commercialization of food products based on market demand, the project will use self-financing mechanisms which should enable women entrepreneurs to maintain their level of services, training and a common set of national standards. The latter will be kept in line with international quality regulations for processed foods, which will increase the confidence of local consumers and improve the prospects for exports.

Women entrepreneurs in the food processing sector in Thailand

In 1996, a needs assessment mission to Thailand was conducted with the aim to integrate the UNIDO Training Programme for Women Entrepreneurs in the Food Processing Industry into the GTZ (German Technical Co-operation Agency) 'Small-Scale Agro-Industrial Development Project' (SSAID). The objective of the project is to promote small-scale agro-industrial enterprises. The activities involve four northern provinces, out of which Phitsanulok and Sukothai were selected for the needs assessment. The project is executed by the Department of Industrial Promotion (DIP), which has offices in all provinces.

The needs assessment consisted of analysis of the training needs of women entrepreneurs in the food processing sector, assessment of training institutions and the running of test TOT and test training of participants.

In Thailand, the Department of Agricultural Extension (DOAE) supports the formation of women's groups in rural areas throughout the country in order to alleviate poverty and offer off-farm activities. These women's groups operate food processing enterprises as a 'joint venture' and receive support from the DOAE in terms of advice, marketing (the produce is often collected by the DOAE and sold in government shops), equipment, and so on. Naturally, some women's groups are better organized than others. In principle, there are two kinds of women's groups: (1) the groups which process and market as a group and (2) those who process individually and use the group only to market their produce or apply for assistance.

In addition to the women's groups, individual food processors have also been interviewed in order to get some idea of how to operate in market conditions, without support from the government. The women interviewed covered a range of food processing activities, for example, soy bean sauce, fish sauce, banana chips and paste, toffee making and pork skins.

The women's groups have some common characteristics, including:

o they were recently established (between 1991 and 1995);
o the number of members varies between 12 and 59 (although some members may not be active in the processing activities); and
o most women's groups have started a saving scheme to accumulate interest and funds for operational costs and investments.

For both the women's groups and the individual entrepreneurs, the production place is the private house or the backyard. Simple equipment is widely used and locally manufactured. The availability of equipment was not considered a problem, however exposure to and information on equipment was requested. Packaging materials, such as plastic bags and containers and glass jars, are easily available, although costly if not bought in bulk. In general, the production and education level of the individual entrepreneurs was higher than those of the women's groups. The average education level is four years of schooling and the average age between 30 and 50. Many have family members who have migrated to Bangkok, leaving the responsibility for agricultural production with the women.

Problems of the food processors

The problems encountered by the women's groups as well as by individual entrepreneurs were similar. The major problems encountered were management related (e.g. marketing, accounting and costing) and technology related (e.g. the need to diversify, the lack of up-to-date equipment and the low quality of the products).

The analysis of training needs could be covered by the UNIDO training programme, while the technology manual needed to be fully revised to cover the food products for the Thai market. In Thailand, food is an important issue and there is a large variety of all kinds of food products and processes. Compared with other

Women work together to produce and package banana chips (G. Herrmann)

countries, the food processed on a small-scale and micro-level is already advanced in terms of packaging and labelling. Based on a market assessment and on the availability of raw materials, the following food products were selected for the training: tamarind sweets, paste and juice; mango paste; chilli paste; pickled vegetables; pumpkin chips; banana chips; soya/mung bean sauces; fermented fish; dried fish; fish sauce; fish powder; sweet shredded pork and 'khaiyiawma' (salted eggs in soda ash).

Test training

The aim of the test training was to test the applicability and the level of the UNIDO training programme and to introduce the participants to the participatory training approach. Due to time limitations, only the training module on the business plan was used. This module was translated into Thai. First, a two-day test training of trainers was carried out with ten trainers (management trainers and food technologists) from different training institutions in the province. Secondly those trainers conducted a two-day test-training with 16 women food processors, women's groups and individual entrepreneurs.

The training for both groups comprised the introduction to the training subject, group exercises, short presentations by the participants, and the use of participatory training methods ('energizers', games, ice-breakers, etc.). An evaluation was carried out at the end of each training day.

This was a very useful exercise for all involved. The level of the training programme was just right; however, major problems were encountered with the translation. Thus it was decided to have the training programme translated by professionals with a background in food processing and grass-root management.

As a result of the assessment, it became clear that training in management and marketing are the most needed subjects. The technology and processing training is already covered by different institutions, although improvement in certain areas (product quality, hygiene, upgrading technologies) is needed too. Therefore, new modules for selected food processes and technologies using the methods of the training programme need to be developed. Criteria for the selection of participants, such as entrepreneurial spirit, business idea, organization of the group and market potential of the food product selected, have been set.

Presently, the training modules have been adopted and translated into Thai and TOT and training courses for participants are under preparation in the provinces of Phitsanulok and Sukothai. In future it is planned to extend the training courses to other provinces. The institutions involved are the DIP as a co-ordinating body, the DOAE for the implementation of the training programme with the co-operation of colleagues and NGOs in terms of providing resource persons and training facilities.

Further reading

'Final report on a needs assessment mission on the formulation of a training programme for women entrepreneurs in the food processing industry', Gabriele Herrmann (1996) GTZ (German Technical Co-operation Agency).

Bibliography

Food processing

Cereal processing: food cycle technology source book, UNIFEM, 1994, Intermediate Technology Publications (ITP), ISBN 1853391360, 72pp.
This book focuses on the processing of four cereals – maize (or corn), rice, sorghum, and wheat. Topics include harvesting, threshing, storage, milling, hulling, baking and fermenting. This book is also available in Spanish.

Dairy processing: food cycle technology source book, UNIFEM, 1996, ITP, ISBN 1853393355, 72pp.
This book outlines traditional methods of processing milk to produce cheese, butter, yoghurt and other milk products, and discusses how hygiene and quality control can be improved.

Drying: food cycle technology source book, UNIFEM, 1995, ITP, ISBN 1853393088, 50pp.
This book is an introduction to the principles of drying and gives an indication of the range of technologies available, along with case studies examining the use of improved drier designs.

Fish processing: food cycle technology source book, UNIFEM, 1993, ITP, ISBN 1853391379, 96pp.
This source book describes the traditional methods of fish processing and then looks at new and improved techniques which in most cases can be constructed locally. Types of processing covered include drying, salting, smoking and fermenting.

Food processing technology, Fellows, P.J., 1993, Woodhead Publishing.
A standard text on all aspects of food processing.

Fruit and vegetable processing: food cycle technology source book, UNIFEM, 1993, ITP, ISBN 1853391352, 72pp.
Offers the non-specialist an insight into the range of methods and equipment available for preserving products, increasing the quality and range of foodstuffs.

Preservation of fruits and vegetables, Lal, G., Siddappa, G.S., Tandon, G.L., 1986, Central Food Technology Research Institute, India, 488pp.
A comprehensive guide to fruit and vegetable preservation at both cottage and commercial scales.

Integrated food science and technology for the tropics, Ihekoronye, A.I. and Ngoddy, P.O., 1985, Macmillan Press Ltd.

Oil processing: food cycle technology source book, UNIFEM, 1993, ITP, ISBN 1853391344, 48pp.
Offers guidance on the selection of appropriate equipment for small businesses, with case studies and technical information about each type of machine.

Packaging: food cycle technology source book, UNIFEM, 1996, ITP, ISBN 1853393347, 48pp.
This book looks at traditional and mechanized packaging systems for use by small-scale producers. Case studies from around the world examine the introduction of improved packaging technology.

Processing and preservation of tropical and sub-tropical foods, Maud Kordylas, J., 1990, Macmillan Education Ltd, ISBN 0333468457, 414pp.

This publication is an invaluable core textbook for students of food science, food technology, economics and domestic science. Different methods of processing and preserving such as freezing, dehydration, fermenting, curing, smoking and canning are given detailed consideration.

Root crop processing: food cycle technology source book, UNIFEM, 1993, ITP, ISBN 1853391387, 76pp.
Covers the most common processing techniques for the major root crops including potato, cassava, sweet potato, yam and other edible aroid crops.

Small-scale food processing: a guide to appropriate equipment, Edited and introduced by Fellows, P. and Hampton, A., 1992, ITP, ISBN 1853391085, 176pp.
Provides information on the major food-processing technologies, divided by food group, including sugar confectionery, milk, meat and cereal-based products. Catalogues the necessary equipment, manufacturers and product details, and prices.

Storage: food cycle technology source book, UNIFEM, 1995, ITP, ISBN 1853393096, 35pp.
This book focuses on the storage of the staple commodities such as grains and root crops, but it also covers other major food groups such as oils, fish, fruit and vegetables.

Technical manual on applied food processing: Technical Cooperation Programme, Caribbean Agro-industrial Development Network, Baciagalupo, A., 1986, FAO Office for Latin America and the Caribbean, 378pp.
This technical manual has been elaborated to exchange practical and successful technologies for small farmers and rural communities. It covers processing of agricultural crops; basic infrastructure required by rural agro-industries; hygienic aspects in small processing plants and the promotion of rural agro-industries.

Tomato and fruit processing, de Klein, G., 1993, TOOL, ISBN 9070857316, 106pp.
This book is written for people who are interested in starting, supervising or financing a small-scale enterprise for processing tomatoes and fruits into juice, jams and jellies. The techniques are low-cost and applicable to many different situations.

Traditional cheesemaking: an introduction, Dubach, J. (translated by Bill Hogan), 1989, ITP, ISBN 0946688435, 112pp.
Using traditional cheesemaking methods, this book gives an idea of the opportunities that cheesemaking offers as a source of rural employment, and of the problems that will be encountered by anyone planning to start such a business.

Traditional foods: processing for profit, Fellows, P.J., 1997, ITP, ISBN 1853392286, 288pp.
This is a comprehensive guide to the processing of traditional foods, from Asia, Africa and Latin America, which are made and sold at a small commercial scale of operation. It provides technical information needed by small food businesses to introduce or upgrade their processes and products, and also serves as a suitable guide for new enterprises in the correct production of foods.

Try drying it! Case studies in the dissemination of tray-drying technology, Axtell, B. and Bush, A., 1991, ITP, ISBN 1853390399, 86pp.
Shows how improving on the traditional techniques of drying by sun and air can provide income-generating activities for groups in the developing world. Examples from Peru, Colombia and Bangladesh; with detailed technical appendices.

Women's roles in technical innovation: food cycle technology source book, UNIFEM, 1995, ITP, ISBN 185339307X, 88pp.
Women's indigenous technical knowledge and innovative solutions to problems are in evidence across the whole range of food

cycle technologies. This book highlights the broad range of expertise that exists in rural areas. The book first gives a brief account of women's indigenous technical knowledge, and its extent.

Training

A participatory systematization workbook, Selener, D., Zapata, Z. and Purdy, C., IIRR.
Systematization is a continuous process of participatory reflection about projects involving both staff and participants. It looks first at how to analyse projects, then how to draw lessons from this analysis which can help to improve the project as it continues.

Colecion de 8 manuales Capacitacion en Agroindustria Rural. (Series of training manuals on rural agro-industry.) PRODAR-IICA, Costa Rica.
These manuals are a useful consultation tool for people involved in rural agro-industry. The methodologies have been specifically developed for projects with small farmers and have been put into practice in countries such as Colombia, Costa Rica, Chile, Ecuador, Nicaragua, Panama, Canada and France. For easy access to the required information, there is a user's guide which enables rapid identification of the required methodology, according to the project's objectives. Furthermore, a series of support tools for the selected methodology are included to enable: the undertaking of research studies; the identification, selection and assessment of project ideas; the analysis and evaluation of production processes; the development of processes and products; technical, economic and financial evaluation of projects; project implementation; the implementation of pilot projects; the multiplication and commercial expansion of projects.

Marketing strategies – training activities for entrepreneurs, Kindervatter, S. and Range, M., OEF International, USA, ISBN 0912917083, 65pp.
This book provides a means for women to solve their marketing problems and increase business profits.

Opening the marketplace to small enterprise, de Wilde, T., Schreurs, S. and Richmond, A., 1991, IT Publications, ISBN 1853390933.
Addressing three fundamental issues – how to find financial support, how to improve products, and how to access markets – this describes proven innovative answers to the obstacles facing small enterprise, together with entrepreneurial case studies.

Participatory learning and action: a trainer's guide, Pretty, J., Guijt, I., Thompson, J. and Scoones, I., 1995, IIED, ISBN 1899825002, 268pp.
This is an excellent and comprehensive guide to the whole subject of PLA. It is well designed and easy to read and use. It covers a wide range of topics, from warm-up exercises with newly formed groups, to adult learning and the challenges of training in the field.

Participatory rural appraisal: practical experiences, Nabasa, J., Rutwara, G., Walker, F. and Were, C., 1995, NRI, ISBN 0 859543927, 52pp.
This booklet provides a very straightforward introduction to the use of participatory exercises.

Training for transformation, Hope, A. and Timmel, S., 1996, Mambo Press, ISBN 1853393533, 462pp.
There are three manuals in the series. First printed in 1984, they provide an excellent introduction to participatory development and are full of practical ideas, suggestions, case studies and exercises.

Training trainers for development: conducting a workshop on participatory training techniques, CEDPA, 1994, PACT Publications, 92pp.
Intended for use by trainers in organizations working in development, who will find ideas

here to help prepare them to conduct participatory training of trainers in their organization. The book uses interactive, learner-centred methods based on the research of human resource development experts such as Malcolm Knowles, Paulo Freire, Gordon Lippit and Leonard Nadler.

Training and teaching: learn how to do it, Bekkering, W., 1992, TOOL, ISBN 9070857251, 90pp.
Discusses guidelines to help an instructor prepare for a teaching assignment and make the lessons both useful and worthwhile. *Training and Teaching* presents a series of lessons, using schematic lesson models and a number of practical building blocks.

Business development

Doing a feasibility study: training activities for starting or reviewing a small business, Kindervatter, S. (ed.), 1987, OEF International, USA, ISBN 0912917075.
A step-by-step guide on starting and reviewing a small business.

Improve your business workbook, Dickson, D.E.N. (ed.), 1986, ILO, ISBN 9221053407, 94pp.
Aimed at small retailing, wholesaling, manufacturing and service businesses, and containing eight sections: buying and selling; manufacturing and service operating; bookkeeping; costing; marketing; management accounting; office work; and planning.

Improving small-scale food industries in developing countries, Edwardson, W. and MacCormac, C.W. (ed.), 1986, IDRC Publications, ISBN 0889363986, 167pp.
This book reviews a variety of experiences in the application and evolution of a small enterprise-oriented process improvement methodology and suggests modifications and improvements.

Marketing strategy: training activities for entrepreneurs, Kindervatter, S. and Range, M., 1986, OEF, 65pp.
One problem area that entrepreneurs themselves identify again and again is marketing. This book provides a means for women entrepreneurs to solve these problems and increase their business profits.

Metodologias Para la Promocion y Evaluacion de Proyectos y Productos de Agroindustrias Rurales. (Methodologies for the promotion and evaluation of food processing programmes.) Boucher, F., Riveros, H. and Castaneda, M., 1995, IICA, ISSN 05345391, 339pp.
This guide provides information on how to evaluate rural agroindustrial enterprises.

Monitoring and evaluating small business projects: a step by step guide for private development organizations, Buzzard, S. and Edgcomb, E. (ed.), 1992, PACT, ISBN 0942127005.
Explains how to document and control progress and how to apply the methods to actual situations, as well as forms, graphs and business procedures to enable implementation. Also included are case studies and a bibliography.

Planning guide for small food and agricultural businesses, McGill University, IICA PRODAR, 1992, San Jose de Costa Rica.
This guide is aimed at those promoting small-scale agro-industrial projects in base communities. The guide is an easy-to-use resource for the formulation of funding requests and in project identification and planning. It also includes a wide list of reference materials to consult for more specific themes.

Small business in the Third World, Harper, M., 1984, J Wiley, ISBN 0471904740.
This book deals with methods of promoting new, small enterprises and with the role of small business in social and economic development. It shows how large businesses can profitably promote indigenous enterprise.

Starting a small food processing enterprise, Fellows, P.J., Franco, E. and Rios, W., 1996, ITP, ISBN 1853393231, 128pp.

This book brings together important aspects of both the technological and business skills needed to start and operate successfully a small food processing business. The emphasis is on thorough planning before the enterprise is established and then careful control of production to minimize costs and maintain the desired product quality.

Where credit is due: income-generating programmes in developing countries, Remenyi, J., 1991, ITP, ISBN 1853390798, 144pp.
Development economics reveal that thousands of poor microentrepreneurs are able to work, invest, and overcome poverty when given the chance; the author looks to the use of credit-based income generation schemes as a new poverty-alleviation strategy.

Management and finance

Basic accounting for small groups, Cammack, J., 1992, Oxfam, ISBN 0855981482, 64pp.
A step-by-step guide to basic accounting and financial management techniques for those with no previous experience of accounting and bookkeeping, this book is ideal for any small group which needs to keep accurate records of its financial transactions.

Consultancy for small businesses, Harper, M., 1977, IT Publications, ISBN 0903031426.
This manual is the result of a six year experiment to provide an economic on-the-spot advisory service to small businesses in developing countries. It provides some solutions to the perennial problems of small-scale entrepreneurs.

Entrepreneurs handbook, Technonet Asia, 1981, IT Publications, 282pp.
A guide for organizations responsible for entrepreneurship development, with chapters on entrepreneurial self assessment, planning and organizing a business, marketing and financial management, and other essential topics.

How to read a balance sheet, Halsall, J.J.H., 1985, ILO, ISBN 922103898X, 216pp.
A programmed learning text, with sections on assets, liabilities, solvency, and liquidity. This edition has been revised to cover recent developments in accountancy, such as inflation accounting.

Manual of practical management for Third World rural development associations, Vol. 2. Financial management, 1989, IRED.
The manual is addressed primarily to grassroots managers and people responsible for conducting, managing and inspiring non-governmental development associations in the Third World.

Quality assurance

Fundamentals of quality control for the food industry, Kramer, A. and Twigg, B.A., 1962, AVI Publishing Co.

'HACCP in street vending in developing countries', Bryan, F.I., 1993 in *Food Australia*, Vol. 45, No. 2.

Hazard analysis critical control point evaluations, Bryan, F.I., 1992, WHO.

How to HACCP, an illustrated guide, Dillon, M and Griffith, C., 1995, MD Associates.
This book is designed to help small businesses gain an insight into practical aspects of food production management systems. It includes step-by-step coverage of HACCP system development; illustrations and diagrams to explain HACCP and decision trees for the identification of significant hazards and determining critical control points.

Manuals of food quality control, Vols 1–9, FAO Publications, Rome, Italy. (Vol. 3: *Commodities*, Martin, P., 1979, ISBN 9251008442; Vol. 4: *Microbiological analysis*, Refai, M.K., 1979; Vol. 5: *Food inspection*, 1984; Vol. 6: *Food for export*, Dhamija, O.P., 1979; Vol. 7: *Food analysis*, 1986 – general techniques, additives, contaminants and composition; Vol. 8: *Food analysis*, 1986 – quality, adulteration and tests for identity; Vol. 9: *Introduction to food sampling*, 1988).

Quality assurance for small-scale rural food industries, Fellows, P., Axtell, B. and Dillon, M., 1995, FAO Publications, ISBN 9251036543, 120pp.
The purpose of this publication is to stimulate greater awareness among small- and medium-scale food processors of the need to reduce risks from pesticides, food poisoning, lack of hygiene and poor manufacturing practices in food processing establishments.

Sanitation and hygiene

Affordable water supply and sanitation, Pickford, J., Barker, P., Coad, A., Dijkstra, T., Elson, B., Ince, M., and Shaw, R. (ed.), 1995, IT Publications, ISBN 1853392944.

Codes of hygienic practice of the Codex Alimentarius Commission, Joint FAO/WHO Food Standards Programme, FAO.
No. 1: Canned fruit and vegetable products (CAC/RCP 2, 1969); No. 2: Code of hygienic practice for dried fruits (CAC/RCP 3, 1969); No. 3: General principles of food hygiene (CAC/RCP 1, 1979).

Food poisoning and food hygiene, Hobbs, B. and Roberts, D., 1987, Edward Arnold Ltd, ISBN 0713145161.

Making safe food, Fellows, P. and Hidellage, V., 1992, ITDG.
This booklet is intended for use by extension workers and trainers in food processing. It is suitable for use as training material and includes posters to remind producers of good manufacturing practice.

Safe drinking water, Howard, J., 1979, Oxfam Technical Guide.

The food hygiene handbook, Sprenger, R.A., 1996, Highfield Publications, ISBN 187191275X.

Packaging materials and labelling

Appropriate food packaging, Fellows, P. and Axtell, B., 1993, TOOL Publications, ISBN 9070857286.
Looks in detail at food and packaging; types of food and prevention of deterioration; packaging materials, filling and labelling; production, re-use and recycling of packaging; implications of introducing packaging; benefits and costs of food packaging.

Community development

Communication skills for rural development, MacDonald, I. and Hearle, D., 1984, Evans Publishing via IT Publications.
A practical companion for those who advise local people to help themselves at agricultural and technical colleges and universities.

Developing technologies for the rural poor, Biggs, S. and Grosvenor-Alsop, R., 1984, IT Publications.
This selective review looks at case studies where NGOs have been involved in rural/agricultural technology programmes directed at the rural poor, and attempts to identify those common features which characterize successful agencies.

How to run a small development project, Geneva Group, 1986, IT Publications, ISBN 0946688478.
This will help the managers of development projects to design and manage their projects well, in particular by emphasizing the importance of forward planning. Covers both starting up and running projects, and working with Northern partner organizations.

Adult learning

Adults learning, Rogers J., 1971, Penguin Education, ISBN 0140802436.
Will prove invaluable to adult-education teachers, many of whom have had no professional training, and to anyone who is planning to enrol for a class or who is simply interested in the process of learning.

How adults learn, Kidd, J.R., 1977, Association Press, New York, ISBN 0809618753.
This comprehensive book on adult learning includes the factors that motivate adults to learn, the physical and sensory capacity of adults, their intellectual capacities and the theories of learning and how this relates to adult learning.

Institutions that support small-scale food processing training

Africa

Botswana
Botswana Technology Centre, PO Bag 0082, Gaborone, Botswana.

Ethiopia
Food Research and Development Centre, Ethiopian Food Corporation, PO Box 5688, Addis Ababa, Ethiopia.

Gabon
Institute de Recherche Technologique, BP 14070, Libreville-Akebe, Gabon.

Gambia
Gambia Food and Nutrition Association (GAFNA), PO Box 111, Banjul, Gambia.

Ghana
Ghana Regional Appropriate Technology Industrial Service (GRATIS), PO Box 151, Tema, Ghana.
Technology Consultancy Centre (TCC), University of Science and Technology, Kumasi, Ghana.

Kenya
Approtech, PO Box 10973, Nairobi, Kenya.
Kenya Industrial Research and Development Institute (KIRDI), PO Box 30650, Nairobi, Kenya.
Technoserve, PO Box 14821, Nairobi, Kenya.

Malawi
Malawi Enterprise Development Institute (MEDI), PMB 2, Mpnela, Malawi.
Small Enterprise Development Organisation of Malawi (SEDOM), PO Box 525, Blantyre, Malawi.

Namibia
Development Centre for Research Information Action in Africa (CRIAA), 22 Johan Albrecht Street, Windhoek, Namibia.

Nigeria
International Institute of Tropical Agriculture (IITA), PMB 5320, Ibadan, Nigeria.

South Africa
Council for Scientific and Industrial Research (CSIR), PO Box 395, Pretoria 0001, Republic of South Africa.
INFRUITEC, Private Bag X5013, 7599 Stellenbosch, Republic of South Africa.

Sudan
Food Processing Research Centre, Khartoum, Sudan.
Intermediate Technology (IT) Sudan, PO Box 4172, Khartoum, Sudan.

Tanzania
Small Industries Development Organisation (SIDO), PO Box 2476, Dar-es-Salaam, Tanzania.
Tanzania Food and Nutrition Centre (TFNC), Department of Food Science and Nutrition, World Health Organisation, PO Box 977, Dar-Es-Salaam, Tanzania.

Uganda
Uganda Manufacturers Association, PO Box 6966, Kampala, Uganda.
Lugogo Show Grounds, PO Box 6966, Kampala, Uganda.
Midway Centre, PO Box 6966, Kampala, Uganda.

Zimbabwe
Intermediate Technology (IT) Zimbabwe, PO Box 1744, Harare, Zimbabwe.
Ranche House College, 87–89 Rotten Row, PO Box 1880, Harare, Zimbabwe.

Asia

Bangladesh
Intermediate Technology (IT) Bangladesh, GPO Box 3881, Dhaka 1000, Bangladesh.
Mennonite Central Committee (MCC), GPO Box 785, Dhaka 1207, Bangladesh.

India
Academy of Development Science (ADS) Kashele, Karjat Taluka, Raigad District, Maharashtra 410 201, India.
Action for Food Production (AFPRO), C52, ND South Extension II, New Delhi 16, India.
Agriculture and Processed Foods Export Development Authority (APEDA), 6 Bhikaji Cama Place, New Delhi 66, India.
Central Food Technological Research Institute (CFTRI), Mysore 570 013, Karnataka, India.
Small Industries Research Institute (SIRI), PO Box 2106, New Delhi 110007, India.
Society for Development of Appropriate Technology (SOTEC), 182 Civil Lines, Bareilly, Uttar Pradesh, India.

Indonesia
Bandung Institute of Technology, PO Box 276, Bandung, Indonesia.

Nepal
Centre for Rural Technology, PO Box 3628, Kathmandu, Nepal.
Development Consultancy Services (DCS), PO Box 8, Butwal, Nepal.
Intermediate Technology (IT) Nepal, PO Box 2325, Kamaladi, Kathmandu, Nepal.

Sri Lanka
Ceylon Institute of Scientific and Industrial Research, PO Box 787, 363 Bauddhaloka, Mawatha, Colombo 7, Sri Lanka.
Industrial Development Board (IDB), 615 Galle Road, Moratuwa, Sri Lanka.
International Centre for Training of Rural Leaders, Yodagama, Embilipitiya, Sri Lanka.
Intermediate Technology (IT) Sri Lanka, 5 Lionel Edirisinghe Mawatha, Kirulapone, Colombo 5, Sri Lanka.

Thailand
Food Technology Laboratory and Institute of Food Research and Product Development, Kasatsaart University, both at 196 Phahonyothin Road, Bangkok 10900, Thailand.
Thailand Institute of Scientific and Technological Research, 196 Phahonyothin Road, Chatuchak, Bangkok 10900, Thailand.

Caribbean

Antigua
Chemistry and Food Technology Division, Ministry of Agriculture, Fisheries and Lands, Dunbars, Antigua, West Indies.

Cuba
Centro Nacional De Inspeccion de la Calidad – Ministerio Industria Alimenticia, Martires 91, Frexes y Marti, Holguin 80100, Cuba.

Haiti
Petites Soeurs de L'Incarnation, BP 1594, Port au Prince, Haiti.

Jamaica
Grace Technology Centre, 7 1/2 Retirement Road, Jamaica.

Europe

Austria
United Nations Industrial Development Organisation (UNIDO), PO Box 707, A 1011, Vienna, Austria.

France
Groupe de Recherche et d'Échanges Technologiques (GRET), 211–213 Rue La Fayette, 75010 Paris, France.

Germany
Association for Appropriate Technology (FAKT), Gansheidestrasse 43, D-70184 Stuttgart, Germany.
German Appropriate Technology Exchange (GATE), Postfach 5180, D-6236 Eschborn 1, Germany.

Italy
Food and Agriculture Organisation (FAO), Via delle Terme di Caracella, 00100 Rome, Italy.

Netherlands
Agromisa Foundation, PO Box 41, 6700 AA Wageningen, Netherlands.
Technical Centre for Agricultural Rural Co-operation (CTA), Postbus 380, 6700 AJ Wageningen, Netherlands.
International Agricultural Centre (IAC), 11 Lawickse Allee, PO Box 88, 6700 AB. Wageningen, Netherlands.
Royal Tropical Institute (KIT), PO Box 95001, 1090 HA Amsterdam, Netherlands.
Technology Transfer for Development (TOOL), Sarphatistraat 650, 1018 AV, Amsterdam, Netherlands.

Switzerland
International Labour Organisation (ILO), International Labour Office, CH 1211 Geneva 22, Switzerland.
OS3, Import-U Informations stelle, Byfangstrasse 19, Postfach 69, 2552 Orpund, Switzerland.

UK
Intermediate Technology, The Schumacher Centre for Technology & Development, Bourton Hall, Bourton-on-Dunsmore, Rugby, Warwickshire, CV23 9QZ, UK.
Midway Technology Limited, St Oswald's Barn, Hay-on-Wye, Herefordshire, HR3 5HP, UK.
Natural Resources Institute (NRI), Central Avenue, Chatham Maritime, Kent, . ME4 4TB, UK.

North America

Canada
International Development Research Centre (IDRC), Box 8500, 250 Albert Street, Ottawa, ON K1G 3H9, Canada.

USA
Appropriate Technology International (ATI), 1724 Massachusetts Avenue NW, Washington DC, 20036 USA.
Post-Harvest Institute for Perishables Information Centre, University of Idaho Library, Moscow, Idaho 83843, USA.
Technoserve, 49 Day Street, Norwalk, Connecticut 06854, USA.
United Nations Development Fund for Women (UNIFEM), UN Plaza, New York, NY 10017, USA.

South America

Bolivia
La Sistematica, Casilla 5474, Cochabamba, Bolivia.

Costa Rica
Centro de Investigaciones en Tecnologias de Alimentos, Universidad de Costa Rica, CP 2060, Costa Rica.
Cooperative Program for the Development of Rural Agroindustry in Latin America and the Caribbean (PRODAR), IICA, PO Box 55-2200, Coronado, Costa Rica.

Guatemala
Centro de Estudios Mesoamericanos sobre Technologias Apropriadas (CEMAT), Apartado Postal 1160, 28 Avienda 18–80, Zona 10-01010, Ciudad de Guatemala, Guatemala.
Institute de Nutricion de Centro America Y Panama, Calzado Roosevelt Zona 11, Apartado Postal 1188, Ciudad de Guatemala, Guatemala.

Peru
Intermediate Technology (IT) Peru, Casilla Postal 18-0620, Lima 18, Peru.

South Pacific

Papua New Guinea
Food Technology Section, Appropriate Technology Development Institute, University of Technology, Private Mail Bag 793, Lae, Papua New Guinea.

www.ingramcontent.com/pod-product-compliance
Ingram Content Group UK Ltd.
Pitfield, Milton Keynes, MK11 3LW, UK
UKHW050544150426
5217IPUK00026B/2070